moneyLOGIC

money LOGIC

FINANCIAL STRATEGIES
FOR THE SMART INVESTOR

MOSHE A. MILEVSKY, Ph.D.
with Michael Posner

Stoddart

Published in 1999 by Stoddart Publishing Co. Limited
34 Lesmill Road, Toronto, Canada M3B 2T6

Distributed by General Distribution Services Limited
325 Humber College Blvd., Toronto, Ontario M9W 7C3
Tel. (416) 213-1919   Fax (416) 213-1917
Email Customer.Service@ccmailgw.genpub.com

03   02   01   00   99   1   2   3   4   5

Canadian Cataloguing in Publication Data

Milevsky, Moshe Arye, 1967–
Money logic : financial strategies for the smart investor

ISBN 0-7737-3171-7

1. Finance, Personal.   2. Investments.   I. Posner, Michael, 1947–   .
II. Title.
HG179.M518   1999   332.024
C98-932923-2

Cover design:
Design and typesetting: Kinetics Design & Illustration

Printed and bound in Canada

To my wife, Edna Ida

CONTENTS

ACKNOWLEDGMENTS

This book would have been impossible to produce without the inspiration and motivation of many friends and colleagues. Each of the chapters that follow is the result of research projects that I have worked on, am working on, or hope to work on with various colleagues in and around the Schulich School of Business at York University. With that in mind, I would like to thank my co-researchers, both past and present, for their insight and ideas. Specifically, they are Narat Charupat, Kwok Ho, Sharon Kim, Steven Posner, Eliezer Prisman, Chris Robinson, Tom Salisbury, and Hans Tuenter.

In addition, I would like to thank Scott Anderson, Lowell Aronoff, Pat Chiefalo, Glenn Daily, David Fowler, Aron Gottesman, Nelson Isabel, François Nault, and Georges Monette for commenting on the various chapters as they were being created.

I would also like to thank the team at FMG, especially the boss, who many years ago hired an eager 13-year-old for a summer job in modern finance — he's been hooked ever since.

On the business side of things, I would like to thank my agent David Lavin at the DLA for introducing me to my wonderful co-author and urging me to undertake this project while arranging all the details — both big and small. This let me tend to what I love best, which is the research.

The editorial staff at Stoddart deserves a distinct mention, with special thanks to Marnie Kramarich for her marvellous assistance with the manuscript.

Finally, I cannot find the words to thank my beautiful and talented wife, Edna Ida, for her unconditional love, patience, and tolerance over the years. In addition to the millions of other things she does so successfully, she found the time to read, critique, and guide each and every chapter.

MOSHE A. MILEVSKY

*God does not play dice
with the world.*

— ALBERT EINSTEIN

INTRODUCTION:

What Are the Odds?

A few months ago, I walked into my local Chapters bookstore and counted three full bookshelves devoted to the subject of personal finance and investment counselling. The book topics covered the complete spectrum — how to pick good stocks, how to choose mutual funds that pick good stocks, how to select a financial planner who will help you choose a mutual fund that will pick good stocks. There were books on mortgages, minimizing taxes, maximizing estates, managing RRSPs, and winding down RRIFs. In total, I found more than 50 books offering financial planning advice to Canadians.

So why, you are perfectly entitled to ask, am I writing another book on personal finance?

The answer is that I'm not. Certainly, it's not a personal

finance book of the ordinary kind. Let's get this straight right away. This book will not help you pick the next Microsoft, or avoid the next Bre-X. This book will not tell you how to find the next superstar mutual fund manager, nor will it identify which mutual fund will be the top performer in the next quarter. This book will not tell you the cheapest place to live, the real estate properties that are most likely to appreciate, or the tax shelter that is least likely to disappear.

I won't pretend to tell you any of that because, quite frankly, I can't. The simple truth is that none of us can accurately predict the future. The future, like the weather, is completely random.

You may recall that until about 25 years ago, your local weather outlook consisted of a simple categorical prediction of whether it would be sunny, cloudy, rainy, or snowy. Statements such as "today it will rain," "tomorrow will be sunny," or "Thursday morning it will snow" were as sophisticated as the reports ever became. Of course, most weather forecasters got it wrong, and the art of weather prediction, which seemed to be based largely on *The Old Farmer's Almanac*, never garnered much respect.

But then, in the mid-1970s, things started to change. Hand in hand with the developments of modern computer technology and the success of the scientific method, the art of weather prediction matured into the science of weather forecasting. Now, you can turn on the weather channel in the morning to learn about a given day's probability of precipitation (POP). Weather forecasters and their computers use what they know about the science of meteorology to convert today's temperature, humidity, and atmospheric pressure into tomorrow's probability of rain. You take the POP and make decisions accordingly.

Technically speaking, the probability of precipitation tells you the chances of it raining more than 0.02 millilitres in a particular region. A 100% POP for today basically means that you can expect it to rain and you should definitely take your umbrella and raincoat to work. A 0% POP means that the sky is completely clear and you can rest assured that it will not rain today. Any number above 0%, of course, represents a greater likelihood of rain. The higher the number, the greater the chance of precipitation. As such, weather forecasters now have more flexibility. They don't have to make definitive predictions, which almost always end up being wrong. Instead, they can focus on the probability. Hence, if today's POP is 40% or higher, you would probably carry an umbrella. If the POP is lower than 40%, you'd probably leave it at home. The decision about whether or not to take the umbrella takes into account the essential uncertainty of the weather and your attitude to risk. The very conservative crowd might tote an umbrella whenever the POP is higher than 10%. Those who can handle a bit of rain-risk will have a higher POP threshold.

Why am I going on in this fashion about the weather? Because the underlying theme of this book involves precisely the same concepts of decision, uncertainty, and risk. You, the investor, often face a choice between two mutually exclusive courses of action — to take an umbrella (i.e., a financially conservative action) or not. And you must make the decision right now, knowing full well that in a day or a week or a month, you may regret not having made exactly the opposite decision.

Many financial decisions are like that. They consist of an either/or component, where each outcome is uncertain, hindsight is 20/20, and the regret is painful. Should I invest in safe certificates of deposits at the bank or should I invest in the stock market? Should I buy universal, whole-life life insurance or should I buy renewable term? Should I pay down my mortgage or should I contribute to my RRSP?

Should I roll my maturing GIC over for another year or should I invest in an index-linked GIC?

Obviously, you want to make these decisions armed with as much information as possible. The more you know, the better the odds that you won't experience loss and regret down the road.

This book is about helping you make informed decisions. More specifically, it's about using scientific methods to examine the odds involved in personal financial decisions. It's about selecting a course of action that will maximize your long-term satisfaction. Of course, when the dice is finally rolled, you may still experience regret. Nothing is ever guaranteed. But at least you will have done the best you could do with the information you had.

Let me give you an example of how to examine the odds in the context of personal finance.

Imagine you've just received a windfall inheritance from a distant relative, or you've won the lottery. You decide to pay off some bills and, having done so, you discover that you still have $10,000 left over. You don't really need the money right now, so you decide to put it away for a rainy day.

You call up your financial adviser and ask: "What should I do with the $10,000? Should I put it all into the Canadian stock market? Or should I play it safe and buy a GIC at the bank?"

Of course, the prudent response on the part of your financial adviser or investment broker would be to suggest some form of diversification; after all, he or she might say, you don't want to put all your eggs in one basket. Depending on your risk tolerance, long-term goals, and financial position, you should probably split the money into various piles and certainly not restrict yourself to the all-or-nothing bank deposit or stock market choice.

But let's examine the all-or-nothing question in greater detail, focusing on the two extreme alternatives. If you "take the plunge" and invest the $10,000 in the Canadian stock market, what are the odds that you will regret this decision? What is the probability that the Canadian stock market is the wrong place to invest your money?

In a sense, you may have noticed, those questions are really pointless. They are pointless because no meaningful answer can be determined unless we specify an appropriate investment holding period. If you take the plunge, will you regret the decision tomorrow? Will you regret the decision in one year? Will you regret the decision in 10 years?

When do you need the money?

Figure I.1 illustrates what I call the time-adjusted "probability of financial regret." Over a one-year time horizon, it shows that there is a 40% chance that a diversified portfolio of Canadian equities will underperform the after-inflation rate of return from the safe GIC bank deposit. Thus, if you're going to need the money in one year, there's a 40% chance that taking the Canadian stock market plunge is the wrong investment and the wrong decision.

But what if you won't need the money for 10 years? In that case, the chart shows that a diversified portfolio of Canadian equities has just an 18% probability of shortfall.

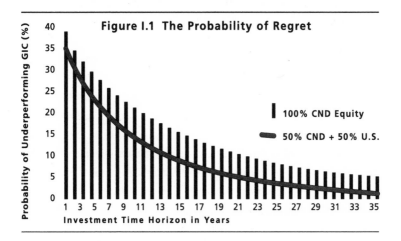

Figure I.1 The Probability of Regret

100% CND Equity

50% CND + 50% U.S.

Probability of Underperforming GIC (%)

Investment Time Horizon in Years

In other words, there's a better than four-in-five chance that, over the next decade, the Canadian stock market will experience a rate of return that is greater than the return currently available from a secure GIC bank deposit. Please note that, as we will see in later chapters, the probability of actually losing money in the Canadian stock market — getting less than your original principal back after 10 years — is considerably lower than 18%; it's about 5%. Think back to the rain example. If the probability of getting half an inch of rain is 20%, the probability of receiving an entire inch of rain is clearly less than 20%. Similarly, to beat the bank deposit, the stock market must work a lot harder than to simply give you your money back. In fact, to get a return of principal, the stock market doesn't have to work at all.

But we are not content with just the return of principal. Our regret benchmark is much higher. We want to beat the risk-free investment alternative, which is the bank deposit. We want to look back with hindsight and feel that we did the right thing.

Finally, what if your time horizon is 35 years away? In this case, the chart indicates a probability of financial regret of roughly 5%. As the time horizon increases, the probability of shortfall decreases rapidly; scientists like to say that it decays exponentially. It never actually hits zero — there are no guarantees in life — but it gets very close to zero. As we shall see later in the book, time and financial risk are intricately intertwined.

Why is time so important? Let me give you an analogy. Let's say that a police officer stops you on the highway. He says you were clocked at 130 km, and have broken the law. He starts to write you a ticket. Is the ticket justified? Well, that depends. If you were driving 130 km per hour, you were going too fast and you deserve the speeding ticket. If, on the other hand, you were driving 130 km per three hours, you were driving much too slowly, in which case you will probably get the ticket for holding up traffic! The point I'm trying to make is that, by itself, the number 130 km is meaningless. To give it genuine meaning, we must know the appropriate unit of time.

In a similar manner, financial risk has an embedded dimension of time. It is meaningless to talk about whether or not something is risky or safe without addressing the relevant time horizon and the financial alternatives. Indeed, over a one-year horizon, the Canadian stock market is clearly quite risky — relative to the secure alternative of putting the money in a GIC. That's because the probability of shortfall, or regret from investing in stocks, is 40%.

On the other hand, if you adopt a 35-year horizon, the Canadian stock market is quite safe, relative to the GIC alternative. That's because the probability of regret would then be about 5%. The flip side of this implies a strong probability of success, of having made the right choice. That probability is close to 95%.

In fact, I would argue that over a 35-year horizon, the GIC, or the money market fund, for that matter, is the risky asset class and the Canadian stock market is the safe asset class, especially when you look at it on an after-tax basis.

Now, you might choose to split your original $10,000 into two parts, investing $5,000 in the Canadian stock market and $5,000 in the U.S. stock market (both parts, of course, invested in a well-diversified equity portfolio). In Figure I.1, you can see that a portfolio consisting of 50% Canadian equity and 50% U.S. equity has a consistently lower shortfall probability than a portfolio of 100% Canadian equity. In fact, over a 20-year horizon, the Canadian portfolio incurs twice the shortfall probability. In other words, it's twice as likely that you'd experience regret going exclusively the Canadian route.

Again, the point I'm trying to make is that you should

examine the odds that are attached to various courses of action.

That's exactly what we'll do in the following pages. I want to help you examine the odds for choices you face in your day-to-day financial life. Among other topics, the book will investigate and focus on the following subjects:

CHAPTER 1
What are the odds that your wonderful mutual fund manager was just lucky?

CHAPTER 2
Should you invest according to dollar-cost averaging or invest in one lump sum?

CHAPTER 3
Should you buy a segregated mutual fund sold by an insurance company or should you stick to a regular mutual fund?

CHAPTER 4
Should you diversify internationally?

CHAPTER 5
Should you roll over your maturing bank GICs or re-invest the funds in the new products known as index-linked (ILGICs)?

CHAPTER 6
Can you create downside protection yourself, by "cooking" financial products like ILGICs at home?

CHAPTER 7
Should you borrow money to invest in a Registered Retirement Savings Plan (RRSP)? Should you pay down your mortgage or invest in an RRSP?

CHAPTER 8
At retirement, should you shift your investments into safe, income-producing assets or should you maintain some exposure to the stock market?

CHAPTER 9
At age 69, should you collapse your RRSP into a life annuity or should you convert it into a Registered Retirement Income Fund (RRIF)?

CHAPTER 10
What is financial risk?

The common factors in all of these questions are the elements of decision, risk, and uncertainty. As you can imagine, you can mount a well-argued case for each side of the coin, but you can't act until you know the actual odds.

This book will help you determine the odds, and let you decide if you need to take the umbrella.

I hope you enjoy — and profit.

How Well Did Your Fund Really Do?

Congratulations! You just received your quarterly or monthly mutual fund statement in the mail and, miracle of miracles, you've actually made a few dollars. In fact, since the last time you checked, your investment has earned quite a handsome return. If this keeps up, you say to yourself, you might be able to retire at age 55 and sail around the world in that yacht you've always wanted.

You're just about to compliment yourself and/or your financial planner on a wonderful choice of mutual fund — and perhaps even send the fund manager a bouquet of fresh chrysanthemums — when you ponder an innocent question: How well did the competition do? After all, who among us doesn't find it far more enjoyable to make money when you know that everyone else hasn't made as much?

So you check the mutual fund rankings from your favourite financial newspaper and find that the median fund in that category earned a full three percentage points less than your fund over the last 12 months. Indeed, over the last quarter, your fund beat the median fund by 1.5% (or 150 basis points). Now you are definitely ready to celebrate. True, a few funds did perform somewhat better than yours, including one that had been recommended to you; you're slightly annoyed to see that it's the top-ranked fund in that category. But you're not greedy. You beat the average. You picked a good, solid fund, run by a skillful manager, and you did well.

Or did you?

The questions you might be tempted to ask are: What are the odds that your fund's fine performance was simply a fluke? What are the odds that you were simply lucky? How can you tell — in a scientific fashion — if your fund manager actually turned in a stellar performance or if he or she (and you) were simply the beneficiaries of enormous good fortune?

Those are the questions I will try to answer here. Specifically, I will examine the issues that you should consider when trying to distinguish true fund-management skill from random, good luck.

Demonstrating genuine and consistent skill in fund management is, I submit, a very difficult art. Let me explain why I think so. The challenge most fund managers face in outperforming the passive stock indices — and the reason for my skepticism of claims of any future ability to do so — is exemplified by the following statistics. According to PalTrak, a Canadian-based mutual fund analysis system, a total of 373 mutual funds (as of September 30, 1998) were classified with a mandate to invest in diversified Canadian equities. Of those 373 funds, however, only 63 have been in existence long enough to have a 15-year track record. The performance record of these 63 mutual fund veterans has varied widely. The best of them earned a cumulative return of 410% over the 15 years. An investment with this top-performing superstar would have effectively quintupled your money. The worst performance record of the 15-year veterans was a cumulative return of 44%. Which also might seem pretty good, until you remember that 44% over 15 years did not even beat the consumer price index inflation rate; over the same period, it would have eroded 55% of your money's value. I don't even want to get into what taxes, transaction costs, and front- or back-end loads would have done to the remainder.

So the range for these 63 players was 44% to 410% during the 15-year period. Moreover, the median fund — half fell above and half fell below — in this category earned approximately 230%. But here is the crux: the passive (no-brainer) TSE300 index earned 250% over exactly the same time period. This is a full 20% more than the median return for the 63 funds. Furthermore, if you examine the individual performances of these 63 funds, you will see that 37 of them were unable to beat the same TSE300 index. In other words, 59% (37/63) of the funds with 15-year track records underperformed the TSE300 index. Only 41% of the funds still active on September 30, 1998, were able to beat the passive benchmark. Clearly, then, the historical odds of beating the index are not great.

Now, granted, some of you may question the comparison of these funds to the broad TSE300 index. Indeed, some of these funds were investing in only a small segment of this market. But believe me, you could perform a similar analysis with any index that you deemed appropriate. The fact is that no matter what index you use — the TSE100 or the TSE35 — the numbers are quite similar. Much fewer than half of the players beat the (appropriate) index averages. Part of this result can be explained by the transaction costs involved with mutual funds, costs which a passive index does not incur. But the margin of underperformance is still too large.

With similar implications, the same story applies to those funds with a 10-year record. The same pool of 373 diversified Canadian equity funds includes 113 funds with a 10-year track record. Over this shorter time period, the best cumulative performance was 323% and the worst performance was –44.3% (yes, that's a negative number). The median return of these 113 funds was 109%. Yet the TSE300 index over the same decade earned a cumulative return of 125%; that's 16% better. Furthermore, only 40 (35%) of those funds beat the TSE300 index; the remaining 65% lagged the index. This is even worse than the 59% who failed the benchmark in the 15-year case. Certainly not comforting.

I suspect that when a fund has a consistently appalling or embarrassing performance record, its sponsors try to kill it — by either merging it with a more successful fund, changing its mandate, or simply closing it down. What this means to you as an investor is that the 63 funds with 15-year track records are a small portion of the much larger universe of mutual funds that once hoped to create their own impressive 15-year track records — and *gave up trying*. In other words, the 63 funds are merely the survivors of the gruelling mutual fund wars. And what you're looking at, therefore, is a biased group of funds.

It's like saying that the average Boston marathon runner completed the race in two hours 47 minutes. Sure, those who *completed* the course did it in two hours and 47 minutes on average. But what about all those runners who dropped out? Clearly, the survivors have better records than the dropouts or losers. What this means for mutual funds is that the *true* 15-year performance record of all those funds that initially tried to create one (finish the marathon) is much worse than that of the survivors. The *true* median for this larger group is certainly lower than 230%.

Looking ahead, I interpret this data to mean that *your* odds of finding a fund that will outperform benchmark averages over the next 15 years are even lower than recorded history would suggest.

Now, please don't get the wrong impression. I am most certainly not against buying or investing in mutual funds. I invest in them myself because, among other numerous benefits, they reduce transaction costs and expenses by pooling purchases. And for those investors who don't have the time to search for good stocks, mutual funds do the job for them.

However, and here is my pitch, I don't necessarily invest in mutual funds with the intention or hope of beating the competition. I also put a fund's performance record through a battery of tests — some of which you will read about below — before I am willing to convince myself that the manager was not just lucky.

Now, you may wonder at this point, does it really matter? After all, the past is history. The fact is, you did well. The fund's performance was better than average. Who cares why?

Well, this is where I respectfully disagree. If the past can be attributed to mere chance, then there is really nothing intrinsically adroit or wise or skillful about your fund manager. More importantly, there is no guarantee that this great performance will be repeated. Of course, even if your manager *has* been skillful, there is certainly no guarantee that this skill will continue. But if your manager is diagnosed as just lucky, then your chance of repeating success — of beating the competition again — is basically 50–50.

With this in mind, I would argue that the "Monday morning quarterback" diagnosis is extremely important when it comes to making decisions about future investments. If your manager is diagnosed as having above-average stock-picking skills, you're likely to feel more comfortable entrusting him or her with even more of your hard-earned money. Certainly, you won't feel as bad paying those high management expense ratios (MERs). If, on the other hand, it's simply luck, you will probably think twice.

In order to make this discussion more concrete, let's consider an example.

You have invested in a European equity fund, which has a mandate to select large capitalization stocks from any industry on the European continent. Roughly speaking, there are 25 mutual funds available in Canada that fall into this category. The best-performing fund in the group (the one your friend Sam recommended to you) had a return of 27% over the last year, while the worst-performing fund in the group earned a return of –8% over the last year.

What does this mean? It means, first of all, that the performance range was 35% — i.e., anywhere from –8% to 27%. Furthermore, the median — or average — mutual fund in the group returned 14%. By median, I mean that half the funds (12 of them) earned less than 14%, while the other half (12 of them) earned more than 14% over the last year. Finally, it means that your fund, which (we'll assume for purposes of this example) is earning 17%, did 3% better than the group's 14% median.

Before we dive into the technical details, a few general statements are in order. Clearly — and you certainly don't need me to tell you this — the longer and the more consistently your fund performs above the average, the more justified you are in considering your fund manager a skillful stock picker. In other words, one good year does not imply any remarkable skill, especially if all the other years were lousy.

Warren Buffett and Peter Lynch, among other famous investors, have demonstrated astonishing stock-picking skills, and have been phenomenally consistent over long periods of time. There is no question that their performance must be attributed to investment acumen; it cannot be dismissed as mere lady luck. The question at hand is: How long — and how far above average — must a fund manager's successful record be before we can declare him or her as having turned in a performance that transcends the realm of chance?

At this point I need to declare a bias. Given the enormous competition that exists in the marketplace, and given the sheer number of individual analysts and institutions that are searching for undervalued stocks, I am somewhat skeptical about *anyone's* ability to consistently beat the market, to consistently do better than average. Somewhere between 60% and 70% of all mutual funds — depending on the period reviewed — fail to beat the stock market averages in the long run. In plain English, *consistently successful* stock picking is a very tough job, and my hat goes off to those who truly manage to outperform.

Let me clarify what I mean. There are 300 stocks in the TSE300 index. Think of it for the moment — please forgive the gambling analogy — as the equivalent of 300 horses at the local racetrack. From this list of 300, Canadian mutual fund managers pick between 30 and 50 of their favourite and most promising stocks, and claim to have superior skills and insight. Why, then, do most of them — as anyone can see from quarterly mutual fund rankings — deliver fund performances that are worse than the market-value average performance of those same 300 stocks?

Even when you account for transaction costs, fees, and commissions, the typical fund manager *still* underperforms the stock market averages. This is not like professional sports, where any athlete in major league baseball, say, can hit, run, and throw better than you and I could ever hope to. It appears that we have many professional fund managers, analysts, stockbrokers, and traders who simply can't — or don't — do better than your ordinary investor who picks a collection of random stocks from the Toronto Stock Exchange and other international markets. In no other professional association can you find so many members who fail to display the basic skills on which the association is founded.

Why?

The reason for this is simple: The members of this association — principally, stock analysts — are competing fiercely against each other to locate hidden and undervalued investments.

The one who succeeds must succeed at the expense of all the others, who failed to locate the same undervalued investment. The one who gets there first must win at the expense of all the others, who were too slow out of the gate.

Now, as the number of active stock analysts increases, and the number of mutual funds expands, the odds of this happening — consistently, I might add — will continue to decline. This fact goes a long way toward explaining the growth of such passively managed investment products as index funds and TIPS (see Chapters 5 and 6), which are available on the Toronto Stock Exchange and have a simple mandate to match or replicate the market average. With the odds of successful outperformance continuing to decline, many investors feel that if you can't beat 'em, join 'em.

Ironically, in the very long term, if too many investors become disillusioned, shift their wealth, and adopt passive investment strategies that simply mimic the broader indices, there will be fewer analysts actively searching for value and the possibility of outperformance — or of finding neglected values — will once again increase.

Therefore, if I have a bias — and I do admit one — it is that I don't believe in the widespread existence of such enduring stock-picking skills. To be convinced of true talent in this field, I require compelling evidence. It is not very different from the scientist who begins with an underlying hypothesis — or assumption — about the world at large. To invalidate the hypothesis, the scientist must uncover strong evidence that is inconsistent with the hypothesis and that cannot be attributed to chance alone.

My personal bias is known — and referred to by economists — as the Efficient Market Hypothesis. The EMH, as it is sometimes known, postulates that markets are efficient in the sense that it is very difficult or even impossible to consistently earn above-average investment returns without taking on excessive levels of risk. We will get to the risk issue in a moment.

Consider the following analogy. Your youngest daughter, your precious eight-year-old, is having her birthday party next week. In addition to all the usual elements, like cake, balloons, etc., you decide to hire the latest fad in children's entertainment — the professional CoinTosser. Although his fee is a little steep, the CoinTosser promises to make your party a memorable one by repeatedly tossing a coin in the air and consistently getting heads. No doubt, you think, he'll have the kids and adults oohing and aahing.

But there's a minor problem with hiring the CoinTosser. Although the province tightly regulates the industry — CoinTossers must attend some classes and pass exams — there are, unfortunately, quite a few charlatans masquerading as professionals. These impostors claim to be able to toss many heads but, when push comes to shove, they disappoint the audience. Of course, they always manage to toss *a few* heads, but with far too many tails in between. But all of the CoinTossers, you have observed, are great marketers. Their advertisements are glitzy. They spend a small fortune on brochures, print ads, and television campaigns, and their fees continue to increase each year. Very few of them, however, seem to possess real, unchallengeable skills.

Being a perfectionist, you decide to interview a few of them before hiring one for your party. More specifically, you ask them to provide their historical track record of coin tosses at other parties so that you can determine whether they are truly adroit CoinTossers or just lucky.

In fact, to make the interview process more scientific, you ask your next-door neighbour, Tom the Mathematician, to provide you with the "chances" of coming up with a specific number of heads when a coin is tossed 10 times. This way, you can determine whether or not the CoinTosser possesses genuine skill.

Tom shows you the following table, and then explains how to read and interpret the numbers. For example, the probability of never getting heads when you toss 10 coins — in other words, tails every time — is 0.00098. That's slightly less than a one-in-a-thousand chance of throwing tails 10 times in a row.

Similarly, the probability of flipping eight heads — not necessarily in a row — when you toss a coin 10 times is

Table 1.1

Tossing a Coin 10 Times

Number of Heads Tossed	Probability
0	0.00098
1	0.00977
2	0.04394
3	0.11719
4	0.20508
5	0.24608
6	0.20508
7	0.11719
8	0.04394
9	0.00977
10	0.00098

*The numbers should add up to exactly one, because all 11 possibilities are enumerated.

0.04394. This, Tom explains, is slightly more than a 4% chance. Clearly, the most likely outcome is five heads, which has a 0.24608 probability, or roughly a 25% chance of occurring. Notice the symmetry: the odds of flipping eight heads are the same as the chance of flipping two heads (i.e., eight tails). They are both 0.04394, about 4%.

You are now ready to interview the CoinTossers. Some are older, and have performed at many parties over the years; others look like they just graduated from college. (The common denominator seems to be that they all wear very expensive clothes.) For consistency and comparison, you ask them to provide the results achieved at their last party.

Candidate Number One comes in with a track record of seven heads — out of 10 tosses — from his last engagement. You look again at Tom's table and see that the likelihood of getting seven heads, out of 10, is 0.11719, which is roughly a 12% chance. According to Tom, this means there's a 12% probability that this CoinTosser's track record is attributable to chance. Stated differently, if a charlatan CoinTosser with absolutely no tossing skills performed this party trick at 100 different parties — tossing 10 coins at each party — then one would expect him to toss seven heads at 12 parties.

The challenge — once again — is to distinguish between authentic skill and mere chance. Your underlying hypothesis is that they are all charlatans — or are simply misguided about their own abilities. To convince yourself otherwise, you require strong evidence. Is seven heads strong evidence? I would say no. Twelve percent is simply too high a number.

So what *is* the threshold? At what probability are we willing to reject our hypothesis and accept the fact that a particular CoinTosser must be quite skilled?

Over the years, statisticians have developed a cut-off point for distinguishing randomness from causality. The number is usually in the 5% region. More stringent cases require a number closer to 1%, and sometimes even 0.5%.

For example, when doctors test a new medical procedure or drug, it is natural for some patients to get better, for others to deteriorate, and for others still to stay the same. Those patients who improve may do so for reasons that have nothing to do with the new medication; in other words, it may just be chance. And those who decline may decline even though the treatment is beneficial. So how does the scientist determine whether to reject the hypothesis that it's all random?

For example, let's say the doctors administered the new treatment to 100 patients. Of these, 60 got better, 20 stayed the same, and 20 declined. How do we know if the medicine was really effective — and that those who improved did not do so simply by chance? To answer the question, doctors use a table that is very similar to Table 1.1. Their table will state the chance that a certain number of patients will get better — or worse — due to purely natural or random reasons. Clearly, the greater the number of patients that improved, the lower the likelihood is of this happening by chance alone.

So the answer, once again, depends on the odds. In the case of a medical procedure, if there is less than a 1% chance of these improvements occurring for natural reasons, the scientist rejects the randomness hypothesis and attributes the outcome to causality — i.e., he concludes that his patients improved as a result of the new treatment. If, on the other hand, the odds of this outcome are greater than 1%, the hypothesis is not rejected. Even though many patients may be better, the scientist cannot be assured that their turn-around was not simply a matter of pure chance, that it was outside the realm of natural randomness.

But you can clearly see the bias. The original hypothesis must be overturned in order to accept the legitimacy of the medical procedure. You can't really prove or disprove a natural assertion of this sort. The best you can do is find evidence that is consistent or inconsistent with your hypothesis.

In the birthday party analogy, the charlatan hypothesis can be discredited only by displaying a very impressive track record. Only then will you accept the fact that your candidates are true professionals and have authentic coin-tossing skills.

For example, if Candidate Number Two shows a latest-party track record of nine heads — according to Table 1.1, this has less than a 1% chance of occurring randomly — you would almost certainly reject the hypothesis that this person is a charlatan. With the first candidate, you could not have the same degree of confidence. Candidate Number One, you'll recall, had a track record of seven heads (a 12% chance) — a number that would not allow you to reject the initial hypothesis that he has no intrinsic skill. Of course, he may in fact be very skillful, and may simply have had a bad day at the last party. But the track record is not enough to change your basic convictions.

Although it may be somewhat harsh to compare mutual fund managers to CoinTossers, the methodology for determining skill is essentially the same.

Remember, many different mutual fund managers and companies are competing for your investment dollars. Some have been in the business for many years. Others are brand new to the game. All implicitly promise — and certainly hope — to do better than their competitors and to beat the market averages. Their historical track records are crucial to their pitch. What should you be looking at? What are the odds that they were just lucky?

The first thing you must do is compare them with the appropriate competition, benchmark, and stock index. If they have a mandate to invest in Canadian resource companies, you (and they) should not be comparing their performance with the financial services sector. Likewise, if they invest only in Canadian stocks, you should not compare their performance with the U.S., Europe, or the Far East.

In many cases, however, the benchmarking comparison is easier said than done. What about balanced equity and bond funds? What about small-cap funds? What about ethical funds? What about funds with a broad investment mandate? What benchmarks do you use to compare, monitor, and confirm their investment skills? Needless to say, these questions are not easily answered. Indeed, a cottage industry of performance consultants has been created to fill this niche. Trustees of public and private pension funds are required by law to monitor the relative — not just absolute — performance of their funds. I can, however, tell you that both fund regulators and consumer advocates are pressuring fund companies and managers to do a better job — in their unitholder reports and initial prospectuses — of telling investors how they performed, relative to the passive and active competition.

In our coin-tossing lingo, if a mutual fund performed better than the index average, I will call that "heads"; if it did worse than the average, I will call that "tails."

Let's say, for the sake of argument, that a fund has been in existence for 10 years — i.e., it has a 10-year track record — and that it performed better than the appropriate benchmark for seven of those 10 years. During the other three years, by implication, it did worse than the benchmark average. Ignoring for the moment the amount or relative magnitude of the over- and underperformance, let's focus on the probability that this performance is consistent with the starting hypothesis of zero stock-picking skill. What are the odds that a fund manager with no skill — but a lot of luck — will be able to outperform the stock market averages for seven out of 10 years?

Once again, Table 1.1 gives us the answer — 12%. Is this number too high or too low? Remember, the lower the number, the more impressive the performance, and the less likely I am to attribute it to chance alone. Therefore, as I argued in the coin-tossing case, 12% is *not* low enough to make me reject my original hypothesis that the performance can be attributed to mere luck.

Now, had the performance been above the average in nine out of 10 years, Table 1.1 would give us a number around 1%, which is very impressive. In other words, if the manager has absolutely no stock-picking skills, the chances of his being above average nine out of 10 years are less than 1%. Such a performance would cause me to reject my randomness hypothesis and declare the manager as having *bona fide* skill.

Of course, there is nothing magical about 10 years. The same approach can be taken with any historical performance record. If a fund has been in existence for 15 years, you can compute the chances of getting 10 above-average years (it's about 9%). Therefore, a fund manager with absolutely no skill can be expected to produce a 10-for-15 track record 9% of the time. Once again, this performance (10-for-15) is not enough in my judgment to reject the randomness hypothesis.

Now, you might ask, why am I so tough to please? After all, a batting average of 10-for-15 isn't exactly bad. In major league baseball, it would be considered a real accomplishment. Why isn't 10-for-15 impressive when it comes to stock picking? Why is my investment bar set so high? Well, remember, you and I would probably bat 0-for-15 against any major league pitcher. But we could probably score a decent 7-for-15 against the stock market averages. That's because the chances are that by simply picking stocks haphazardly, half the time we would do better than the stock market averages, half the time we would do worse. This is why a mutual fund investment average of 10-for-15, though certainly respectable, isn't really that impressive. It definitely isn't enough to overturn my good-luck hypothesis. We must remember the litmus test — how far is this outcome from the no-skill case?

Ten-for-fifteen looks okay until you begin to examine the track record of investment demigods. For example, it's estimated that the legendary Warren Buffett has a 22-for-25 record. This means that he outperformed market averages in 22 of 25 years of investing.

What are the odds of this occurring through mere chance? What are the chances of this occurring if Warren Buffett had no stock-picking aptitude? The answer: about one in 50,000. That, to me, is strong evidence consistent with the premise that he's a talented investor. Of course, true skeptics would argue that every group of 50,000 investors should produce one Warren Buffett on average — simply as a result of chance. But the magnitude of his performance is even more impressive.

This brings me to the many caveats and disclaimers in my simple perspective.

First and foremost, I have completely ignored the amount by which these track records beat or failed to beat the average — i.e., the magnitude of over- and underperformance. There's no denying that the performance of a Warren Buffett or a Peter Lynch is more impressive than their success rate — narrowly defined — would indicate. That's because the amount by which they have outperformed the averages is also inconsistent with a randomness hypothesis.

Indeed, all fund managers who "bat" 7-for-10 are not alike. Some manage to outperform the averages by a large margin. Others barely exceed the benchmark by a percentage point or two. Obviously, the higher the margin, the more likely I am to declare them skillful.

In practice, therefore, we need a table that is slightly

more complicated than Table 1.1. We need a probability table that takes into account the magnitude of the over- and underperformance.

More importantly, a money market fund manager who outperforms the category average by a full percentage point is much more impressive than an international equity fund manager who outperforms the average by 1%. Clearly, the higher volatility in the latter category implies a wide variation in performance with a complementary number of funds doing much better and much worse than average. On the other hand, the very *low* volatility in returns on money market funds, which tend to yield a clustering of performance numbers, makes a 1% margin quite remarkable. Therefore, when examining the magnitude of outperformance, it's crucial to consider — or adjust for — the level of volatility or fluctuations in that particular category. Industry analysts refer to this — and you may have heard the term — as adjusting performance for risk.

Although the underlying mathematics can be daunting, Table 1.2 provides a rough sense of how the outperformance chances stack up. Specifically, and without getting into too much detail, I classify three distinct categories of mutual fund volatility or fluctuation factors: low, medium, and high. You might think of low volatility as a money market or short-term bond fund. Medium volatility might be a balanced fund, comprising both equity and bonds in roughly the same proportions. High volatility corresponds to a pure equity fund, invested both in Canada and internationally. Remember that the lower the volatility, the more impressive is a fixed outperformance margin.

For example, a low-volatility money market mutual fund that manages to earn a one-year return of 6%, when the index average was 5.5%, has exceeded the benchmark by a margin of 50 basis points. The probability of this occurring — assuming that the manager has no particular skill — is

Table 1.2

Volatility of Fund Category

	Low	Med	High
Outperformance Margin			
50 bp*	23.97%	36.18%	42.98%
100 bp	7.86%	23.97%	36.18%
200 bp	0.23%	7.86%	23.97%
250 bp	0.02%	3.85%	18.84%
500 bp	0.00%	0.02%	3.85%
600 bp	0.00%	0.00%	1.69%

* "bp" stands for basis points. One basis point is equal to 1/100 of a percentage point. Statistically speaking, in order of magnitude, low volatility is 5%, medium volatility is 10%, and high volatility is 20%. A probability of 0.00% does not mean that it is impossible, but rather that the number's first four digits are zero.

roughly 24%. Not very impressive. Furthermore, the probability of another "unskillful" manager in the same category earning 6.5% (100 basis points above the average) is a much lower 8%. This number sounds more promising. The lower the probability, the higher the margin of outperformance.

In fact, at some point, the margin gets so high — roughly at 150 basis points for the low volatility fund — that we must reject the hypothesis of randomness and conclude that the manager truly is skillful. This is akin to the CoinTosser flipping nine heads out of 10 — or a fund manager outperforming the index nine years out of 10; in both instances, due to the low probability, we reject the hypothesis of randomness and attribute the performance to skill. In the first situation, we were looking at investment returns over many years, strictly in terms of success and failure. In this case, we are looking at the investment return from any particular year.

Interestingly, the same 100-basis-point margin of outperformance doesn't appear impressive at all when the fund happens to be in the medium- or high-volatility category.

Remember, the lower the probability number, the more impressive the result. In fact, in the medium and high categories, you need a much greater outperformance number before the findings can be dismissed as being attributable to pure chance. In the medium-volatility category, for example, a 250-basis-point margin (and in the high-volatility category, a 500-basis-point margin) is the point at which I would get excited. The reason is simple. High volatility leads to lower levels of clustering in investment returns. As such, there is a greater likelihood of exceeding — and, analogously, falling short of — the benchmarks by higher amounts.

Remember, though, that we are looking at an investment return for a single year. A medium-volatility fund manager who can (a) exceed the benchmark for seven years out of 10, but at the same time (b) outperform the benchmark by 200 basis points in any one year, is performing in a way that is extremely unlikely and highly improbable with no investment skill. Although separately both events (a) and (b) are within the possibility of randomness, the combination of the two events is definitely not.

Bear in mind that I do not want to create a false sense of precision with these numbers. Indeed, simple volatility may not be the only factor to examine when adjusting for risk. Certainly, the margin of outperformance is not the only concern. How tax-effective is the fund? How liquid are the investments? How high are the expense ratios? As a consultant who has worked in this industry, I can assure you that benchmarking and measuring outperformance is a complicated — and many times contentious — process. But the underlying intuition is as follows: True skill is very hard to measure, and the odds should be examined with caution.

CONCLUSION

There are three levels of investment performance to be expected from mutual fund managers. First and foremost — by accepting fluctuating stock market risk — you can unquestionably demand to surpass the long-term rate of return from a risk-free investment in term deposits, Guaranteed Investment Certificates, money market funds, or Canada Savings Bonds.

Second, by entrusting your money to a particular mutual fund company or money manager, it is not unreasonable to request that they toss more heads than tails — in other words, repeatedly do better than the stock market averages. Otherwise, why bother with active management? You could simply buy a passive index investment, or do it yourself by picking your own stocks.

Third and finally, in exchange for those high management expense ratios, front- and back-end loads, as well as other service charges, you should insist that your fund manager outperform the appropriate index averages by a statistically significant margin. In short, any fund manager should display a track record that is undeniably attributable to skill.

With that in mind, you and your financial planner should always be cognizant of the main question: What are the odds that this performance can be attributed to simple chance alone? Remember, the lower the number, the more valuable the service provided by the manager.

Dollar-Cost Averaging:
Pros, Cons, and Myths

Eat healthily, exercise regularly, and invest according to the principles of dollar-cost averaging. I really can't quibble with the first two; the medical evidence is overwhelming. But I do have very serious concerns about the third strategy.

It never ceases to amaze me how popular and wide-spread the practice of dollar-cost averaging has become. According to conventional wisdom, it's the key to a long and prosperous life — the investment equivalent of a healthy diet and regular exercise. Indeed, this mantra has now been repeated in the popular press so many times that it has become virtually axiomatic.

But is dollar-cost averaging really everything it's cracked up to be? My goal in this chapter is to answer that question — to examine the odds of successful dollar-cost averaging and to discuss the narrow conditions under which it makes sense and the many conditions under which it doesn't.

But let me state my bias clearly up front: My personal view, which I will try to support with solid facts, is that many alternative investment strategies give you far better odds than dollar-cost averaging.

For the record, dollar-cost averaging — also known simply as DCA — is a systematic investment strategy in which a fixed dollar amount is invested on a regular basis in a particular stock, mutual fund, or other asset class. For example, many Canadian households, at the encouragement of their financial advisers, have implemented automatic monthly withdrawals from their bank accounts — $250, for example — that go directly into their favourite mutual fund(s).

Now, according to advocates of DCA, this method of forced savings has the benefit of buying more units when prices are lower and fewer units when prices are higher. The same $250 will buy 2.5 units of fund XYZ when it is selling at $100 per share, but only two units of fund XYZ when it is selling at $125 per share. So the cheaper the price, the more units you can buy; conversely, the more inflated or expensive the price, the fewer units you'll be able to acquire. This amounts to the first part of a "buy low, sell high" strategy.

To make DCA look even more impressive, one can demonstrate that after one year of implementing this strategy on a monthly basis, the average cost of the units you've acquired will actually be lower than the average monthly price of the units during the year. Using this approach, you have consistently bought into the fund at a better-than-average historical price.

For example, after a year of investing $250 a month, you have a total outflow of $3,000. That's all you know for certain. The actual *value* of your portfolio — at year-end —

may be higher or lower than $3,000, depending on how the units performed and what they are then worth. But one thing is mathematically guaranteed to be true. The average price you paid for those units — or the value of your portfolio at year-end divided by the number of units you are holding — will always be lower than the average month-end price of those same units. So, if you paid an average of $100 for the units, you can be sure that the average monthly price was higher than $100 over the year. If you paid an average of $150 per unit, you can be sure that the average monthly price was higher than $150. This is a mathematical certainty, because you always buy more when prices are lower and less when prices are higher. Similarly, if you cut down your caviar consumption when it's expensive and eat more when it's cheap, you will always end up paying less for your caviar compared to the average price. This is why the strategy is called dollar-cost averaging. Your investment is averaged into the market — over the course of the year — at a fixed cost each month.

So what, then, you might ask, is wrong with dollar-cost averaging? If you did this for a few years — effectively buying at below-average prices — your investment portfolio would be in very good shape. Wouldn't it?

Well, the answer depends on what you're measuring the strategy against. Compared with not saving or not investing at all, dollar-cost averaging is a wonderful idea. I'm solidly in favour of people taking care of their own needs and saving for long-term goals by putting money away on a regular basis. It's a sensible *modus operandi*. But it makes no sense to blindly recommend a specific financial strategy without looking at appropriate alternatives. Indeed, this philosophy applies not only to dollar-cost averaging, but to any invest-ment tactic. The question then is, what can we use as a comparator to DCA?

Well, I would like to compare dollar-cost averaging with

a natural and symmetric alternative called lump-sum investing — or LSI for short.

For the sake of argument, let's suppose that you have $3,000 in cash, which you would like to invest in equity mutual fund XYZ. However, North American capital markets are (we'll assume) at historically high valuation levels. Accordingly, you are debating whether to (a) invest the entire $3,000 right now in a lump sum, or (b) dollar-cost average the money into the market over the next year. Practically speaking, the DCA strategy would be implemented by placing the $3,000 in a money market fund — or even a simple interest-bearing chequing account — and then transferring $250 each month (plus any accumulated interest), and acquiring as many units as you could afford of equity fund XYZ.

Clearly, by the end of the year — under both strategies — the $3,000, plus or minus gains and losses, will be completely invested in equity fund XYZ. The main issue at hand can be stated as a simple question: Which of these two strategies is better? Is it true — as so many experts claim — that dollar-cost averaging is preferable and wiser?

Before we answer this question, let's make sure we understand exactly how dollar-cost averaging and lump-sum investing would look in practice.

Let's start with your $3,000 investment. The price of one unit of XYZ mutual fund is initially $100. The LSI investment strategy is pretty straightforward. Your $3,000 buys you 30 units ($3,000 = 30 x $100) and you intend to hold them for the long term. At the end of the year, if the price of the unit is $125, you've made a profit of $750 (30 units x $25) on your initial investment of $3,000. That's a 25% return in one year — very respectable indeed — and corresponds to the 25% increase in the XYZ unit price. You participate fully in the percentage increase. Similarly, under LSI, if the price of the unit falls to $75, you lose $750 (30 x $25), and are left with a portfolio valued at $2,250 at the end of the year. Once again, you participate fully in the percentage decrease. One can therefore say that the volatility of your invested capital is equivalent to the volatility of the units.

However, with dollar-cost averaging, things are a bit messier. Now, the $3,000 is split into 12 segments. Each segment is invested — or used to acquire units — on a monthly basis. At inception — for argument's sake, January 1 — the first segment of $250 buys 2.5 units at $100, which is the initial price. The remaining 11 segments are set aside (preferably in an interest-bearing account) to be used in the subsequent 11 months. On February 1, the second segment of $250, plus one month's accumulated interest on that amount, will be used to acquire additional units of XYZ.

Here's where the fun begins. If, on February 1, the value of XYZ units has fallen to $95, the $250 plus interest (say, $251.25, at half a percent per month) will now buy 2.6447 units of the XYZ fund. This is more than the 2.5 units purchased in January, because the unit value has fallen. And the more XYZ has fallen, the greater the number of units you can acquire.

In contrast, if the value of XYZ units increased to $105 by February 1, the same $251.25 will only buy 2.3928 units. This is obviously less than 2.5, because the value of XYZ has increased. So the more XYZ has increased, the fewer units you can acquire with the fixed $251.25.

Indeed, when the unit price increases by 5% to $105, the dollar-cost averaging investor — with only January's capital in the market — gains a meagre 2.5 units x $5 = $12.50 on $3,000, not counting the bank interest. The lump-sum investor, on the other hand, has gained a full 30 units x $5 = $150, which is synonymous with the 5% increase in the fund's value.

The same principle applies on the downside. If the unit price decreases by 5%, to $95, the dollar-cost averaging investor loses 2.5 units x $5 = $12.50 on the original $3,000 investment. The DCA investor's $3,000 has become $2,987.50, a reduction of a mere 0.4% — ignoring any interest from the bank account where the funds are waiting to be averaged in. The lump-sum investor has lost 30 units x $5 = $150, which is 5% of the $3,000, mirroring the 5% loss in unit value.

This phenomenon is widely referred to as the *volatility reduction* of dollar-cost averaging. DCA acts as a shock absorber on both the upside and the downside. As you saw from the example, you don't lose as much from DCA if the price falls, but you don't gain as much if it rises.

The process of buying piece by piece continues each and every month until all the remaining segments — plus any accumulated interest — are fully invested in units of XYZ. This slow yet methodical approach means that you gradually build up an exposure to the units of XYZ. In the meantime, your investment's sensitivity to changes in unit value is much less than one-for-one, until you build up a total exposure to the underlying units; that is, until your capital is completely invested in the units. Indeed, the total value of your equity will not fluctuate (or bounce around) as much as the underlying unit values. This, once again, is the reduction in volatility. Finally, when the 12 months are over, the shock absorbers are entirely removed and you are in the same boat as the lump-sum investor. Except, chances are, the lump-sum investor is in the more comfortable bow and you are in the lagging stern.

Why?

Think about the big picture for a moment. There are three distinct possibilities that could ensue by the end of the year. In the first scenario, the stock price stays relatively flat over this period. In Figure 2.1, this is displayed with the price-path leading to the letter B. As you can see, give or take a few dollars added or subtracted during its journey, the investment ends up at the same place it started — namely, at $100 per unit.

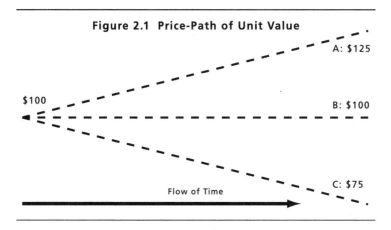

Figure 2.1 Price-Path of Unit Value

A: $125

$100

B: $100

C: $75

Flow of Time

In the case outlined above, both DCA and LSI will yield — or leave you with — roughly the same amount of money at the end of the year. Therefore, I would argue that if you knew with perfect foresight that the behaviour of the investment would be similar to price-path B, it would not matter to you whether you used DCA or LSI. Certainly there would be no particular benefit to DCA, unless the price-path were to wander up and down a great deal on the journey from $100 to $100, in which case DCA would be *slightly* better. But when the price stays relatively constant throughout the year, and there is no high and low to speak of, both strategies leave you with roughly the same amount of money. Buying all your caviar at the beginning of the year isn't any worse or better than buying equal dollar amounts of caviar, when the price of caviar doesn't fluctuate. (Of course, if you could predict price-path B, you wouldn't bother with this investment to begin with.)

But what if the price-path followed a route similar to C in Figure 2.1? Here, the unit value started at $100, but drifted steadily lower, losing a substantial sum of money, and finally ended the year at $75 per unit. In other words, what if you had perfect foresight, and you knew the investment would lose money? Which strategy would you rather follow? Neither, of course; if you knew the value would drop, you'd keep the money in the bank.

But here, a good case can be made for DCA, as opposed to LSI. That's because if you had taken the plunge right at the beginning of the year and had bought all your units at $100, you'd have suffered a loss of $25 for each and every unit. Using dollar-cost averaging, on the other hand, you would have spread your purchases across the year, during which time the cost per unit was declining, and you would therefore have acquired most of the units at a lower price. Although this may not be much comfort in a declining market, the steady drop in value means that, using DCA, you would not have lost as much when the unit price fell to $75 at the end of the year.

So I must admit, following price-path C, the DCA strategy seems the better of the two investment options.

Okay. But what about price-path A? What if you have perfect foresight and just know that the unit value of the XYZ fund will increase from $100 to $125 by the end of the year? With this premonition, would you rather go the DCA or the LSI route? Would you rather buy slowly, or acquire all your units right away? The obvious answer is that the time to invest is when you have the money — buy in as soon as possible.

Clearly, if you knew ahead of time that the unit price would rise over the year, you wouldn't wait to invest. Because if you did, you'd be buying at increasingly higher prices. So here, the DCA approach isn't so impressive. If you adopted it in connection with price-path A, you'd have far fewer units and much less money at the end of the year, compared to LSI.

So let's summarize these three cases. With price-path B,

you're indifferent; with price-path C, you prefer dollar-cost averaging; and with price-path A, you prefer lump-sum investing.

So is it a tie?

No. In fact, this is precisely where the odds come in. As discussed in later chapters in this book, in the very long run, equity-based investments will increase in value. In other words, in the long run, price-path A is more likely to occur than either price-path B or price-path C. Therefore, since A has the highest odds of occurring — and lump-sum investing is clearly the best choice for that scenario — I must conclude that lump-sum investing gives you the better odds.

Of course, there is no denying the existence of bear markets. In any particular year, there's a strong chance that the final price of XYZ units will be described by price-path B or, even worse, price-path C. But once again, I appeal to the odds of regret. What are the odds that you will regret the decision to dollar-cost average, relative to lump-sum investing? If price-path A is more likely to occur than price-path C — and 50 years of Canadian capital markets certainly confirm this — then we must conclude that the odds of regret are lower with a lump-sum investment strategy.

If you dollar-cost average, and price-path A is the norm, then you will suffer an investment penalty. The penalty comes from *not* being in the market, from the beginning of the year.

Remember, though, that short-term money does not belong in the stock market, with or without dollar-cost averaging. If, on the other hand, you are planning a long-term investment, and you want the money to end up in fund XYZ, I would advise you to adopt the lump-sum approach, and forget the hype about DCA. And I would recommend this strategy despite the possibly devastating effect of a market collapse immediately after your single lump-sum investment.

Now, even if you're in it for the long haul, you may still feel uncomfortable about price volatility and fluctuations. Believing that price-path A is more likely doesn't necessarily mean you can forget about risk. Wouldn't dollar-cost averaging help cope with price fluctuations? Wouldn't it mitigate some of the volatility? Maybe, just maybe, the reduced fluctuations are worth the performance price (investment penalty) you pay in lower returns. In fact, isn't volatility reduction the primary justification and rationale for portfolio diversification? You sacrifice some returns, but you sleep better knowing that your investment is less prone to unexpected tremors — to volatility?

It's an interesting argument. And, to be fair, it's a valid one. But in my judgment — and this is the key — the reduction in your return under DCA is more than it should be for the amount of volatility reduction it offers.

What I am arguing is that there are far more efficient ways to reduce volatility — such as diversifying your capital across stocks and money market funds — without incurring the same penalty imposed by dollar-cost averaging. In other words, if the volatility of a lump-sum strategy concerns you, then my advice is to avoid the stock market to begin with. Or, if you're determined to be in the markets, put 56% of your capital into equities (or equity mutual funds) and put the remaining 44% in a lower-risk money account. This 56/44 mix will create the same effect as dollar-cost averaging — i.e., it will reduce your investment volatility and possibility of loss because only 56% is exposed to the more volatile equity market — without incurring as large a performance penalty.

Figure 2.2 provides a graphical illustration of the "problem" with dollar-cost averaging. The horizontal axis displays the volatility or uncertainty in the outcome of the investment strategy, while the vertical axis displays your expected long-term return. The higher you are on the vertical

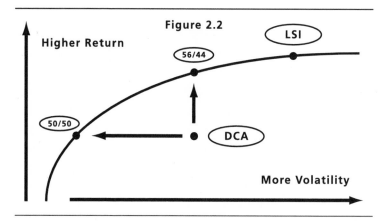

Figure 2.2

axis, the higher is your expected return. Likewise, the further you are to the right on the horizontal axis, the higher the volatility or uncertainty associated with the strategy.

Clearly, lump-sum investing, which is in the upper right-hand corner, provides you with a greater expected return than dollar-cost averaging, but it is more volatile or uncertain. Things can go very well or they can turn very bad. In the same picture, you will notice that dollar-cost averaging has a lower volatility and a corresponding lower expected long-term return. Your return is lower because you are not completely invested in the market at all times, but, by the same token, your volatility is lower.

As an alternative to dollar-cost averaging, I propose a 56/44 mix between the equity fund and the money market fund. The result will be a higher level of expected return, with the same level of volatility. Alternatively, an equally valid strategy is to invest with a 50/50 mix between equity and money market funds. The level of expected return will remain the same, but the volatility will be reduced to a level even lower than that realized under DCA.

It is my opinion that investors who enter the market using dollar-cost averaging to mitigate volatility — and planning to be fully invested by year-end — are exhibiting contradictory behaviour. On the one hand, they want 100% exposure to the market over the long term; on the other hand, they claim to be concerned with short-term volatility. I say: Choose your time horizon and stick to it.

Okay. Perhaps I am waxing too philosophical here.

To get a better sense of what I mean by "reduction in volatility," please look at the following table, imagining that you have $10,000 that you want to invest for the next year, and that you have a choice between a mutual fund and a safe 5%-interest-bearing bank account.

The fund is expected to earn 12.5%, but in any year the return can fluctuate by 20% on either side of that figure.

Table 2.1

Amount allocated to mutual fund*	What to expect at year-end	Your investment's variability
$10,000	$11,250	(+/–) $2,000
$7,500	$11,062	(+/–) $1,500
$5,600	$10,920	(+/–) $1,121
$5,000	$10,875	(+/–) $1,000
$2,500	$10,688	(+/–) $500
$0	$10,500	(+/–) $0
DCA	$10,875	(+/–) $1,121

*Note: The remainder, the portion not allocated to the fund, is invested in the 5% account.

Here is how to read the table. For example, if you invest the entire $10,000 in the mutual fund, at year-end you can *expect* — no guarantees — to have $11,250. This is because the mutual fund is *expected* to appreciate by 12.5% per year. That $1,250, added to your $10,000 investment, will give you $11,250.

However — and this is crucial — mutual fund investment returns are variable. That means, at year-end, that your final return will be in the vicinity of $11,250, *plus or minus* $2,000. The $2,000 corresponds with the 20% volatility of the mutual fund. So, therefore, in all likelihood (actually two-thirds of the time, according to the laws of statistics), you will have between $9,250 and $13,250 at the end of the year. But I reiterate that you can expect $11,250, which is the midpoint of this spread.

In the same manner, you can expect tomorrow's weather to be 25 degrees Celsius, but the variation can be *plus or minus* 10 degrees, for example. Therefore, in all likelihood the temperature will be in the 15- to 35-degree range.

Let's look at another case in the table. If you allocate nothing to the mutual fund, and put all of the $10,000 into the bank account, you can *expect* $10,500 at the end of the year — with no variability. This is simply the 5% interest rate, guaranteed.

Now — here is my main point — what happens if you put the money in the bank and gradually, using the dollar-cost averaging approach, invest your $10,000 in the mutual fund on a monthly basis? In other words, what can you expect at year-end?

Well, the table indicates that you can *expect* to have $10,875 at year-end, but with a variability of *plus or minus* $1,121. So with a DCA strategy, in all likelihood (two-thirds of the time), you will receive between $9,754 and $11,996.

This is where the inefficiency of dollar-cost averaging should become evident. You can see from the table that if you immediately allocated $5,000 to the mutual fund and the remainder to the bank account, you can *expect* to receive the same $10,875 that a $10,000 DCA investment would have yielded. But the variability of your investment would be lower at year-end. As the table shows, the variability of the $5,000-in-fund and $5,000-in-bank scenario is *plus or minus* $1,000, while the variability of DCA is *plus or minus* $1,121.

What this tells us is that you can generate the same expected return provided by dollar-cost averaging — namely the $10,875 — but with lower variability (and therefore lower risk), by simply splitting your money in half. One part goes into the mutual fund, the other goes into the bank account. At year-end, you will have the same amount, on average, as you would have had with DCA, but the level of uncertainty is reduced.

In the same manner — and from a different angle — the table indicates that if you were to invest $5,600 into the mutual fund, you would have $10,920 at year-end, with a variability of *plus or minus* $1,121. This, of course, is the same level of variability that the DCA strategy would have created. But it provides a better return; here, as you will notice, you can *expect* to earn $10,920 – $10,875 = $45 more than you would have received from DCA.

This is why Figure 2.2 has two suggested alternative strategies to dollar-cost averaging: both are more efficient. One strategy (50% in equities, 50% in the bank) gives you lower variability or uncertainty for the same return that DCA would provide; the other (56% in equities, 44% in the bank) gives you greater return — in this case, $45 more — than a DCA approach, with the same amount of variability.

Now, it may be that you don't regard the $45 difference in return as significant. You might be asking, "If all I stand to lose from using dollar-cost averaging is $45 on a $10,000 investment, who cares?"

I can't argue with that. But remember my original agenda. I simply wanted to convince you that there was and is nothing special or magical about dollar-cost averaging. My main point is that you can do just as well — and even a bit better — by not dollar-cost averaging. And that's exactly what this table shows. If you're interested in more of the theory, a great deal of research has been done by economists criticizing and lamenting what they call the fallacy of dollar-cost averaging (see the Appendix for some references).

One of those studies demonstrated quite clearly that

over the last 50 years, a dollar-cost averaging investment strategy would have yielded a worse return than a lump-sum investment strategy with the same level of risk. The researchers identified a long-term performance penalty suffered by dollar-cost averaging, which they estimated at between 1% and 4%, depending on the time period and market involved.

Of course, this fact should come as no great surprise, because the markets have trended upwards — price-path A, remember, was the norm. Consequently, the sooner you get in, the better you fare in the long run. For that matter, discovering the occasional period in history when dollar-cost averaging outperformed lump-sum investing is not exactly proof of its superiority; that's like searching out bear markets and declaring that, for that period, money would have done better under the mattress.

So what, in the end, am I really saying? Only this: If you feel comfortable investing in a way that will lead to an eventual 100% allocation to equity — what DCA would accomplish by the end of the year anyway — then I say create that allocation now. Don't procrastinate. If, on the other hand, you're concerned with the volatility that lump-sum investing will create, then — right now — allocate 56% to equity and 44% to a money market fund and re-evaluate at year-end. Because even that strategy, in my judgment, is better than the piecemeal, 12-segment, DCA approach.

In fact, if you don't have the capital right now, but you do plan to automatically withdraw money each month from your paycheque, I'd recommend that you borrow 12 times that amount, pay it back in monthly installments, and create your desired asset allocation right now. If you have a long-term investment horizon, and are not particularly disturbed by daily fluctuations, go for the total LSI strategy. If the volatility concerns you, pick the 56/44 solution, or some variation thereof. But whatever you do, do it now.

You may have noticed that new versions of dollar-cost averaging have recently been advocated. These entail investing more than $250 — our hypothetical monthly segment — when the unit price has declined since the previous month, and less than $250 when the unit price has increased. The rationale behind this twist is that when something is on sale, you should buy even more than you originally intended, and when things are pricey, you should buy less. (Of course, go figure when things are relatively cheap or expensive!)

But I find this new wrinkle to be just another form of market timing, which is ill-advised for ordinary, small investors, and mostly a loser's game for professionals. Those who can produce evidence of periods in which a particular strategy (this enhanced-DCA, for example) would have worked are probably not telling you about the thousands of other strategies they examined that did not work. Nor can they promise that this one strategy will continue to prevail.

This is known as the "data mining" problem in financial markets. Analysts have access to thousands of days of historical trading data, which they test against hundreds of different trading strategies, hoping to find one that will outperform the market. Indeed, one or two have been found to work well in the past, but these are simply statistical aberrations with no guarantee of persistence. Among the more humorous is the one that claims that in the year when a team from the National Football League's NFC wins the Superbowl, stock markets in the U.S. will move up; the reverse will occur if a team from the AFC wins.

Needless to say, my comments about DCA apply equally to these aberrations as well. The painful thing about this enhanced-DCA strategy is that it deprives dollar-cost averaging of the only unquestionable merit it has — namely, the no-brainer, automatic forced saving that its discipline imposes.

CONCLUSION

I believe that institutionalized dollar-cost averaging is a highly commendable financial counselling strategy because it automatically forces people to save for their long-term goals. Indeed, if they had to rely on their own will power — to save whatever is left over after all the monthly bills are paid — many people would fall short of their financial objectives.

With that in mind, however, one must realize that from a conceptual perspective, dollar-cost averaging is simply an inefficient financial strategy. If you have a lump sum of money that you eventually would like to invest completely in the stock market, you are far better off investing it all right now — what I call taking the plunge — as opposed to going the piecemeal DCA route. Replacing one major gamble (the lump sum) with many smaller gambles (DCA) does not make prudent financial sense.

Ah, but what if the market falls right after you've taken the plunge? Well, if you're not comfortable with that prospect, if the market's volatility scares you, or if you fear the dramatic short-term possibility of loss, then you're probably not psychologically suited for total equity exposure. And if that's the case, then from a risk-and-return perspective, you're far better off partitioning your wealth — right now — between stocks and less volatile financial instruments, and holding both for the long term.

In sum, those who hesitate, lose. The odds are you will do better financially by avoiding dollar-cost averaging. But please don't forget to eat healthily and exercise regularly!

Segregated Mutual Funds:
What Is the Value of a Guarantee?

Segregated mutual funds, or Seg funds for short, have actually been around for many years. But it's only recently that
they have captured the attention of large numbers of
investors. It's estimated that 10% of the Canadian fund
market is now comprised of Seg funds. Indeed, the Seg
fund bandwagon is getting rather crowded; almost every
mutual fund company, it seems, now offers a Seg fund version of its most popular mutual fund. You can now buy
almost any particular mutual fund in two flavours — Seg or
Reg (regular).

But what exactly is a Seg fund? Why are so many people
suddenly buying them? And why do they cost more — in
the form of higher management expense ratios — than regular funds?

The term "segregated" comes from the insurance industry, where these funds originated. There, they were (and continue to be) held separate — segregated — from the other assets of an insurance company. At first glance, Seg funds appear to function just like conventional mutual funds; that is, they consist of a large, pooled collection of stocks and bonds. They are controlled by professional money managers. And they are owned by thousands of unitholders.

As with ordinary mutual funds, Seg fund money managers can and do specialize in particular economic sectors, countries, or industries, and they compete against their colleagues and peers to give you the best possible return on your money. Unit values fluctuate on a daily basis, depending on the performance of the underlying securities owned by the mutual fund. And of course, you can buy and sell (redeem) your units at any time by contacting the fund company, perhaps paying a front-end or back-end load in the process.

There, however, is where the similarities end — and the differences begin.

Seg funds have three essential characteristics, three defining features that distinguish them from regular mutual funds. First, although they look, taste, and feel exactly like mutual funds, they are considered and classified as insurance policies by the federal and provincial authorities. They are governed by the Insurance Act and can only be sold by a licensed insurance agent — unlike regular mutual funds, which can be sold only by a licensed mutual fund salesperson. As insurance policies, Seg funds contain a certain degree of creditor bankruptcy protection that regular mutual funds do not have. If, for example, you are forced to declare personal bankruptcy, your Seg fund will be shielded from your creditors' reach. That's in sharp contrast to conventional fund investments, all of which would be considered part of your assets, and within reach of bankruptcy trustees. Of course, one must bear in mind that a deliberate and fraudulent use of Seg funds to avoid creditors will probably not stand up in court. As a general rule of thumb — for creditor protection to apply — the Seg fund must be purchased at least one year prior to the personal bankruptcy declaration. In some cases, the requirement may be as stringent as five years.

The second distinguishing feature of Seg funds — and far more valuable in my opinion — is the downside, or stock market crash, protection that they provide. By law, Seg funds must promise you at least a 75% return of your original principal; in fact, the new generation of Seg funds has increased that number to 100%. Here is how this novel feature works.

When you buy a stereo or CD player, you are usually told that if the product malfunctions — or even if you are not happy with its performance — in the first 30 or 60 days, you can return it to the store on a full, money-back guarantee. It's as simple as that: You return the product, show your receipt, and they give you back the full purchase price, plus tax.

Well, Seg funds offer a similar money-back guarantee. If you are unhappy with the performance of your investment, you can return the units to the company that sold you the fund and (at least for the 100% Seg fund type) get all of your money back. Your original purchase price will be completely — or at a minimum 75% — refunded.

Clearly, you would only want to return the units to the seller if the unit values have declined in price and you have lost money. If the units now cost *more* than your purchase price, you'd be in the black, and obviously would not want to seek a refund of lesser value. Clearly, too, a 100% guarantee is more valuable than a 75% guarantee. But both types of Seg fund seem to provide a feature that regular mutual funds cannot promise or deliver.

But hold on a minute: Doesn't this guarantee sound too good to be true? How can an insurance or mutual fund company afford such a guarantee? Can it be as easy as returning your units and getting a full — or substantial — refund? It seems suspiciously like the proverbial free lunch, of which investors should always be wary. So what's the catch?

In fact, there are several catches, or caveats. Let's delve into them one by one.

First and foremost, you can't simply return the investment units to the company and demand your full principal back whenever you want, or whenever the fund values are under water. According to the rules, you must wait 10 years from the date of purchase. In other words, if the fund value is under water in 10 years' time, then you can go and ask for your money back. But no sooner.

At this point, you might well be saying to yourself: "Ten years! Why do I have to wait 10 years?" Imagine reading the fine print and being told that if your stereo malfunctions, you can get your money back, but only if you wait for 10 years. Such an offer for a stereo, fridge, or CD player is almost meaningless.

But here's the question: Is this Seg fund money-back guarantee also meaningless? Is it worth anything? After all, what are the odds that in 10 years fund values will be lower than when you bought them? What are the odds that a fund will experience a 10-year compound annual rate of return that is negative? And, for those funds providing only a 75% guarantee of full redemption, what are the odds that the fund will lose 25% of its value over a 10-year period? Not to mention that in 10 years, your $10,000 won't be worth anywhere near $10,000 in today's terms.

As you may recall from the Introduction, the odds are overwhelmingly in your favour. I estimate that the probability that a well-diversified portfolio of Canadian stocks will earn a negative return over a decade is roughly 5%. That means there's a 95% likelihood that your fund will be above its initial value after a 10-year period. However — and this is important to remember — the probability of a negative return is still greater than zero. In other words, there is some chance, even though it is quite small, that you will actually make use of — or exercise — the Seg fund's guarantee.

For example, as of August 31, 1998, the 10-year annualized return from Japan's stock market, as represented by the NIKKEI 225 index, was –4.5% (yes, that is a negative number). This means that if you had invested $10,000 in the NIKKEI 225 stock index on August 31, 1988, 10 years later you would have had only $6,300 left. The –4.5% annualized loss translates into a 37% 10-year loss. This may be an extreme example.

But look carefully at the mutual fund rankings in your favourite newspaper. On August 31, 1998, in the Canadian small-to-mid-cap category, there were 25 mutual funds with a 10-year track record. Of those 25 funds, three had 10-year returns that were negative. In fact, in almost every category — except for money market funds, bonds, and balanced funds — you can locate one fund with a negative 10-year record. It's probably worse than just one or two funds. As I noted in Chapter 1, I suspect that when a fund experiences a consistently negative return, it is merged with a more successful fund or it is closed down. In this way, the horrible record is erased. Economists call this the "survivorship bias" in historical returns.

Hopefully, I have convinced you that the Seg fund's money-back guarantee must have some value. The question is, how much is that guarantee worth, and how much should you pay for it?

As I mentioned, I prefer to think of the money-back guarantee that a Seg fund provides as being like an extended warranty program for your fridge, stove, or car. When you buy these products, you are given the choice of purchasing extended protection. The extended protection can be for five, 10, or 20 years, or even for life. Naturally, this extended protection will not come free; you will have to pay more than just the price of the appliance. If you are financing the purchase, instead of paying the full purchase price outright, you will probably have to make higher monthly payments if you choose the extended warranty program.

Most of us have had to face this sales pitch at some point in our lives. To extend or not to extend? My concern, usually, is that if I reject the extended warranty, the product can be expected to break down the day after the regular warranty expires. Alternatively, if I do take the extra coverage, the product will perform flawlessly and I will have paid all this extra money for nothing. Or, more typically, the extended warranty won't actually cover anything that is likely to happen.

Buying a Seg fund, then, is like buying a regular fund — or Reg fund — with an extended warranty. As with any insurance decision you make, you have to ask yourself two separate questions: How much insurance do I need? How much should it cost?

If the extended warranty is not too expensive, relative to the purchase price of the appliance, I'm likely to buy the extension. If the price is too high, I will turn it down. So how much should an extended warranty cost on a mutual fund?

The way you pay for your Seg fund warranty is via a higher management expense ratio (MER). For example, you can buy mutual fund XYZ without the extended warranty and pay an annual 2% MER. Or you can buy Seg fund XYZ with the extended warranty and pay an extra 1% — the insurance portion — for a total 3% MER.

Every mutual fund has its own particular MER. Some are quite high; some are very low. The same thing happens with Seg funds. Some charge a minor additional fee of a few tenths of a percentage point; others charge an extra 1% to 1.5%. On average, total MERs for Seg funds in Canada are between 2.5% and 3.0%. Equity growth funds are at the high end of the range; balanced funds are at the low end.

I certainly can't tell you whether to buy the extended warranty or not. That's a personal decision and it depends on your lifestyle, goals, and fears. If you use the CD player every day, I would argue that buying an extended warranty might be prudent. On the other hand, the occasional user might never cash in.

What I can do, however, is give you a sense of how much you should be paying for the Seg fund guarantee, and provide some guidance as to when it's likely to be more valuable to you personally.

But before I get into the technical details of what is a reasonable MER surcharge, we need to know about the third and final feature that is unique to Seg funds.

The Death Benefit

In addition to the money-back guarantee available after 10 years, all Seg funds offer another money-back pledge that can be redeemed in the event of death. It works this way: If the owner of the Seg fund (or policy) dies within the 10-year period, the beneficiary of the policy will receive either the current market value of the fund or the original purchase value, whichever is greater. Thus, if the Seg fund has lost value at the time of death, the beneficiary will get a full refund of the original purchase price, even though the 10 years have not elapsed. Moreover, to increase the appeal of Seg funds, the payments go immediately and directly to the beneficiary, without having to go through probate, which can be an expensive and time-consuming process.

Indisputably, this death benefit adds more value to the

10-year guarantee, since there is always a chance that you might die within that decade. Indeed, the older you are, the greater the chances.

The following table illustrates the probabilities of dying during any 10-year period, as a function of your initial age.

Table 3.1

The Chances of Dying During the Next 10 Years

Current Age	Female	Male
30	0.5%	0.9%
40	1%	3%
50	3%	6%
60	9%	16%
70	22%	35%
80	50%	66%

(Source: Statistics Canada 1996; see also chapter notes in Appendix)

As you can see from the numbers, there is a very high likelihood that the 80-year-old will cash in on the death benefit before the 10 years are over. For women, there's a 50% chance of cashing in, while for men, there's a 66% chance. In fact, many companies restrict the sale of Seg funds to people under the age of 80 (and in some instances even age 70), because of the likelihood that the guaranteed death benefit will be invoked within the 10-year period. This likelihood, of course, makes the guarantee more expensive to provide; hence the desire to avoid it, on the part of the insurance company.

As for the 30-year-old, there is almost no chance that the death benefit will be used. Both men and women of that age have less than a 1% chance of dying before their 40th birthday, making it extremely unlikely that the death benefit guarantee would be triggered.

Consequently, 80-year-old females are getting something that is 100 times more valuable than it is for the 30-year-olds. Once again, this is because an 80-year-old female is 100 times more likely than a 30-year-old to use the guaranteed death benefit (and the implicit avoidance of probate). For all other ages, the ratio is somewhere in between. The higher odds of usage make the product more valuable for older people.

In fact, because investors of all ages pay exactly the same expenses in the form of additional MERs, I would argue that young people who buy Seg funds are effectively subsidizing older people who buy Seg funds. This situation is similar to the case in which (non-accidental) life insurance is sold to all ages, and both sexes, for precisely the same price. Here, young females are subsidizing old males. Because the latter group is more likely to die — within any period of time — they are effectively paying less and getting more.

So here is one piece of advice that requires little elaboration. The odds dictate that the extended warranty that Seg funds provide is much more valuable the older you are, especially if you are male. In fact, at age 80, the 10-year guarantee becomes more like an expected three- to five-year guarantee, given the strong possibility of death within that 10-year period. (It's interesting to note that some Seg funds provide a 100% guarantee in the event of death, but only a 75% guarantee after 10 years. This obviously reduces the value of the guarantee, especially to the young.)

So What Is Downside Protection Worth?

That is our central question. What is investment insurance worth? How much should you pay for the right — but not the obligation — to return your investments and get all of your money back?

The first thing to do, when valuing this guarantee, is to estimate the likelihood that the guarantee will be used.

What are the odds that the fund will experience a negative rate of return over the 10-year period? Then, assuming that the fund is in the red in 10 years' time, we must estimate the expected magnitude of the shortfall; that is, we must calculate the amount the insurance company must compensate the Seg fund owner. For example, in the case of a $10,000 Seg fund investment, if the value of your units is $9,000 on January 15, 2009 — 10 years after you bought them — the insurance company will be obligated to pay you $10,000 in exchange for the units. This implies a $1,000 shortfall magnitude; it's the amount that the insurance company loses.

Of course, both the odds and the expected shortfall magnitude will depend on how volatile or risky the underlying fund is. For example, the growth Seg fund category, which invests in riskier common stocks, is more volatile than the balanced Seg fund category, which invests in a more stable mixture of stocks and bonds. Similarly, money market Seg funds are less volatile than balanced Seg funds because they invest in short-term, interest-bearing securities that are unlikely to fluctuate at all. As such, the guarantee provided on a growth Seg fund is more valuable than the guarantee provided on a balanced fund, which in turn is more valuable than the guarantee provided on a money market fund.

That's because "value" is synonymous here with the likelihood and expected magnitude of the guarantee being exercised. Consistent with this volatility ranking, the additional MERs on growth Seg funds are higher than the additional MERs on balanced Seg funds, which are higher than the additional MERs on money market Seg funds. In fact, many people — including some well-known personal finance commentators — even question the wisdom of buying money market or even balanced Seg funds, given the incredibly small likelihood that the guarantee will ever be exercised. I tend to agree.

But let's not confuse the *value* of a guarantee with the

need for a guarantee. I don't mind getting a guarantee, no matter how unlikely it is to be of use to me, provided that it's free or close to it. If I do have to pay for it, I want to be very sure that I'm paying a fair price and, more importantly, that I actually need that type of protection.

Let's focus for a moment on growth Seg funds and how to value the guarantee they provide. Once again, the $10,000 invested today is guaranteed to be there in 10 years or at death.

But remember, $10,000 today is worth much more than $10,000 will be worth in 10 years' time. In fact, at an effective interest rate of 5%, the present value of the $10,000 you'll have 10 years from now is approximately $6,140. Algebraically, we would express this as $10,000 divided by $(1.05)^{10} = \$6,140$.

When only 75% of your money is guaranteed, the calculation should be 75% of $10,000, which is $7,500. Then, to obtain the present value, we divide the $7,500 by 1.05 to the power of 10 to obtain approximately $4,600.

So the first thing to note about this marvellous, full money-back guarantee is that it isn't exactly a full money-back guarantee at all; it really gives you more like 61% of your money back. Or 46% when only 75% of the principal is guaranteed. It's also instructive to compare this rather disappointing result with what your $10,000 of today would have become had you invested in a simple, risk-free bank account. At the same 5%, your money would have grown to $10,000 x $(1.05)^{10} = \$16,288$. This, essentially, is why long-term guarantees of principal are worth much less than short-term guarantees. The present value of the guaranteed amount — $10,000 in this case — declines quite rapidly with the time horizon. It is the *real, present value* of the guaranteed amount that determines the worth of the guarantee, not just the number itself.

Consider another case. Imagine a Super Seg fund — a

complete figment of my imagination — that promises to double your initial investment principal ($10,000), but only at the end of 25 years. If the fund value is under $20,000 in 25 years' time, they will give you $20,000 back — even though you originally invested only $10,000.

Sound impressive? Would you sign up for the Super Seg? I say, no thanks.

Let's run through the numbers again. What is the present value of the $20,000 to be guaranteed in 25 years' time? A simple calculation, at 5%, shows it to be $20,000/(1.05)^{25} = $5,906. This figure is even less than the above-mentioned $6,140, which is the present value of the $10,000 under a normal 10-year horizon.

With these examples in mind, I obtained some actuarial estimates for a Seg fund guarantee. Table 3.2 displays the results. I'll explain in a moment why I include the five-year guarantee, even though no Seg funds currently offer such products.

First, let me explain this table. By volatility, I simply mean the amount by which the fund's value is likely to fluctuate in any one year. On a slightly more technical level, volatility dictates the range around which the fund is likely to fluctuate two-thirds of the time. By Up-Front Cost, I mean the amount one would have to pay out-of-pocket to acquire the downside protection. Of course, when you buy a Seg fund, you don't pay for the downside protection immediately; you pay annually, in the form of higher management expense ratios. Therefore, by Additional Annual MER, I mean the additional amount that you pay every year to fund the guarantee. It's comparable to paying for an extended VCR warranty with higher monthly payments rather than in one lump sum when you first buy the VCR.

Now, let's see what the table tells us. If, for example, you purchase $10,000 of a growth Seg fund that has a 10-year guarantee and an annual volatility of 15%, then the downside protection guarantee that you are getting is worth about $328. If, instead of paying for the guarantee up front, which nobody does, you decide to pay in annual installments in the form of higher MERs, the value is an additional 42 basis points — or slightly more than two-fifths of 1%.

Table 3.2

Value of the Guarantee on a $10,000 Seg Fund Investment*

Five-Year Guarantee

Volatility of Fund	Up-Front Cost	Additional Annual MER
5%	$10.00	23 bp**
10%	$170.00	38 bp
15%	$443.00	99 bp
20%	$757.00	169 bp
25%	$1,086.00	243 bp

10-Year Guarantee

Volatility of Fund	Up-Front Cost	Additional Annual MER
5%	$1.50	0.2 bp
10%	$90.00	11 bp
15%	$328.00	42 bp
20%	$641.00	82 bp
25%	$985.00	125 bp

(Source: See chapter notes in Appendix)

*The price of downside insurance depends on (i) the probability of the event occurring and (ii) the magnitude of the loss, should the event occur. The actual formula that put these two components together is known as the Black-Scholes/Merton formula, named after the people who derived it and who were awarded a Nobel Prize in Economics in 1997. The ingredients include the volatility of the investment and the interest rates in the market, as well as the dividend yield on the underlying investment. The interest rates are important because of the present value arguments that I cited; the dividend yields are needed to compute the benefit from actually holding the investment. For the purpose of our calculations, I used an interest rate of 5.75% and a dividend yield of 1.5%.

**"bp" refers to basis points. One bp equals 1/100 of a percentage point.

Of course, if the fund is more volatile — and you can obtain this information from any newspaper that ranks mutual fund volatility and returns — then the value of the guarantee is higher. This is because the chances are higher, all else being equal, that the fund will experience a loss and the guarantee will be cashed in.

The higher value and cost for the more volatile funds might explain why there are no Seg funds for emerging market, natural resources, and other high-risk mutual funds. The downside protection is simply too expensive, owing to the higher likelihood and greater magnitude of the potential loss.

The value of a guarantee would also be increased if the guarantee period were shorter, and the fund company promised to refund your principal in, for example, five years instead of 10. This is because the fund is more likely to experience a loss over that shorter period, and because the present value of your refund will be higher.

In fact, it's not just an explicit shorter maturity period that makes the guarantee more valuable, but also the *implicit* maturity period. For older people who are purchasing Seg funds, and who are likely to die within the 10-year period, the value of the explicit 10-year guarantee is higher than it is for a younger person. Because they can be expected, on average, to die within five years, their estate will probably cash in on the money-back guarantee earlier. So when you think about it, older people are paying for a 10-year guarantee and getting the value of a much shorter guarantee.

Bells and Whistles

There are two ways to acquire a Seg fund. One is directly through an insurance company; the other is through a mutual fund company that has partnered with an insurer to offer the guarantee. Traditional insurance company Seg funds, which usually provide only the 75% money-back guarantee, are available from almost all insurance companies in Canada. In some cases, the funds are managed in-house, although outside money managers are frequently employed. So, although you may be buying a Seg fund from London Life Insurance Co., for example — with a 75% guarantee in 10 years — you have a choice of funds that are managed by the likes of AGF, Beutel Goodman and Co., Fleming Canada, and other well-known and well-established companies.

As of October 1998, the following mutual fund sellers had hooked up with insurance companies to provide Seg fund versions of their mutual funds, with a 100% guarantee of principal. In these cases, you are presented with a true Seg or Reg decision.

Table 3.3

Mutual Fund Companies Offering Seg Funds with an Extended 100% Warranty

Fund Company	Insurance Partner
BPI Financial	Transamerica Life
Talvest Inc.	Maritime Life
C.I.	Toronto Mutual Life
Trimark Inc.	AIG Life Insurance of Canada
Manulife*	Manulife

Note: Manulife Seg funds are offered via their GIF (Guaranteed Investment Funds) program.

What makes these fund companies different, innovative, and competitive is that some of them provide additional wrinkles to the 100% guarantee. For example, Trimark, BPI, and Manulife, among others, allow buyers of the Seg fund to "lock in" the value of the fund should its value go up during the guarantee period, thus ensuring a higher maturity value. The lock-in automatically resets the guarantee amount at the current market value, so any gains are protected. The lock-in option can be exercised or applied at any time, but is usually restricted to four times a year. This feature of Seg funds can get a bit complicated, so let's look at an example.

On January 15, 1999, you purchase $10,000 worth of XYZ Seg funds; each unit costs $10.00, which means that you own 1,000 units of XYZ. The 100% guarantee implies that — provided you don't withdraw any funds from the account in the interim — 10 years from now, you're guaranteed to get at least $10,000 back. On January 15, 2009, regardless of what the funds are actually worth on that day, you can return your units for the full $10,000 that you invested. Furthermore, if you die during the next 10 years, your beneficiary will get back either the current fund value or $10,000 — whichever is greater.

Of course, if the fund units have increased in value, you are entitled to their market value at that time. Remember, it's only with a market decline, which could put your funds deeply under water, that it would make sense for you to cash in on the guarantee. In other words, don't fix it, if it ain't broke!

Now, let's say, just for the sake of argument, that on July 15, 1999 — six months after you bought the Seg fund units — the stock market is doing well and each fund unit is worth $10.50. This represents a 5% increase, which means that your original investment is now worth $10,500. In theory, you could sell your units right then and there — of course triggering income taxes if they are held outside an RRSP — and book the $500 gain. On the other hand, if you are a long-term investor, you may have no intention of selling right now. Still, it would be nice, you think, to be able to lock in the $500 gain that you just made. You certainly don't want to lose it. You don't want to watch the market slide back down over the next few months and see your handsome $500 in paper profits go up in smoke.

With such thinking in mind, many Seg funds allow investors to lock in their gains by making a declaration that resets the 10-year time frame. In other words, you can contact the fund company and ask them to reset the 10-year clock and protect what is now a $10,500 investment — not just the old $10,000.

Wonderful, you might think. But be careful. Remember, locking in the higher value means that you must reset the clock, so that the 10-year guarantee starts anew. Your old $10,000 investment is guaranteed for 9.5 years; resetting the clock means that you will be pushing the maturity guarantee to July 15, 2009, which is six months later.

In theory, another way to lock in and protect the value of the investment is to sell the fund at its current ($10,500) market value, and then immediately repurchase $10,500 worth of the same units. This would create a new 10-year guarantee on the new $10,500 investment. Of course, this activity would incur transaction costs in the form of loads, fees, and commissions. Even worse, the sale would be deemed a taxable event that would require you to pay income taxes on any capital gains.

Nevertheless, it is important to recognize that the lock-in feature is valuable to the holder *only* because it avoids these costs. There is nothing special about the ability to lock in. In fact, it is probably Revenue Canada that is losing (giving) the most from the lock-in feature because of the lost — better phrased as deferred — income tax. Some Seg funds allow you to switch in and out of funds within the same family; they, like the lock-in feature, provide value only by eliminating fees and deferring taxes.

You are caught on the horns of a dilemma. Should you destroy the old $10,000 guarantee that matures in 9.5 years in exchange for a new $10,500 guarantee that matures in 10 years? Or should you keep the old 9.5-year guarantee, and forget about locking in the new, higher value of your fund units?

If only they would let you lock in the new value, but

keep the old maturity date. That would give you the best of both worlds. But the mutual fund sellers won't let you do that, so you must choose: sooner or higher?

Both horizons may seem a long way off, but there is a serious trade-off here. Of course, if the increase in the fund's value were 20% over six months, to $12 a unit, it's not hard to see that you should lock in the higher value, even though it means you must extend the guarantee period. Conversely, if the increase were only 1% (to $10.10), you'd probably decide not to lock in that figure. But the in-between values are harder to judge.

The following table explores this in-between zone. The numbers are appropriate for a typical growth Seg fund with a volatility of 15%.

Let's explain the table and examine the implications. The numbers on the left represent the amount by which the

Table 3.4

Your Seg Fund Has Increased in Value

Should You Lock In the New Level or Keep the Old Guarantee?

Increase in Value	Time, in Months, Since Last Lock-In						
	3 M	**6 M**	**9 M**	**12M**	**18M**	**24M**	**36M**
0%	No	No	No	No	No	No	No
1%	Yes	No	No	No	No	No	No
2%	Yes	Yes	Yes	Yes	No	No	No
3%	Yes	Yes	Yes	Yes	Yes	No	No
4%	Yes	Yes	Yes	Yes	Yes	Yes	No
5%	Yes	Yes	Yes	Yes	Yes	Yes	No
6%	Yes	Yes	Yes	Yes	Yes	Yes	Yes
7%	Yes	Yes	Yes	Yes	Yes	Yes	Yes
8%	Yes	Yes	Yes	Yes	Yes	Yes	Yes

(Source: Author's calculations, using computer simulations and an option pricing model. See the Appendix as well as Chapters 8 and 9 for details on methodology.)

Seg fund value has increased since the last level was locked in. The numbers range from 0% (no increase) to an 8% increase. Across the top is the amount of time that has passed since the last lock-in was declared. The numbers range from three months to three years.

The amount of time that has passed since the last lock-in, not just the amount by which the market has increased, is very important. This is because the more time that has elapsed, the shorter the remaining time until the original 10-year guarantee is over. For example, if 36 months, or three years, have elapsed since the last lock-in, then seven years will remain until the original guarantee can be used. All other things being equal, locking in after 36 months is more detrimental — or costly — than locking in after three months. In the former you are sacrificing a seven-year guarantee in exchange for a 10-year guarantee. In the latter, you are only sacrificing a 9.75-year guarantee in exchange for a 10-year guarantee.

Here's an example. Let's assume it's been two years since your last lock-in and the fund's value has increased by 3%. In these circumstances, you should not lock in the new level. Technically speaking, the old guarantee — at a unit value that is 3% lower than the current level and which matures in eight years — is more valuable than a new guarantee at the higher current level which matures in 10 years. In contrast, if the fund has increased by 5% since the last lock-in, which was two years ago, you should definitely lock in the new level.

As a general rule, the more time that has elapsed since the last lock-in, the higher the threshold that will be required to request a new lock-in. Likewise, the less time that has elapsed since the last lock-in, the lower the threshold required to induce a new lock-in. In fact, for increases greater than 5%, it is almost always optimal to lock in, regardless of how much time has passed.

Although Table 3.4 only applies to the 15% volatility case, or the standard Canadian growth fund, the results are quite robust — or non-sensitive — to the actual volatility of the Seg fund. In other words, the decision to lock in or not lock in doesn't really depend on how volatile the fund is. Remember, though, the more volatile your fund, the more valuable your actual guarantee.

Typically, of course, there are restrictions on the number of lock-ins that you can request per year, so you don't want to lock in for any minor increase. You should use them sparingly. A full analysis of the circumstances under which you should and should not lock in for all types of Seg funds would keep a team of Wall Street rocket scientists busy for an entire year. Such an exercise is definitely outside the scope of this book. But as you can imagine, it all comes down to the odds.

Given how difficult it can be for investors to make decisions on lock-ins, it's no surprise that some Seg fund sellers have already abandoned the discretionary lock-in feature; now, they automatically increase your guaranteed maturity value each time the market increases. This product is currently being sold by companies affiliated with Maritime Life. As might be expected, it comes with its own distinct wrinkles. For example, they suspend the lock-in feature 10 years prior to the declared maturity value of the investment. Thus, if you buy the Seg fund on January 15, 1999, you must declare a maturity date — let's say January 15, 2115. This Seg fund would then automatically lock in all gains made, without extending the guarantee period, until January 15, 2005, which is 10 years prior to the maturity date.

CONCLUSION

Seg funds differ from traditional (Reg) mutual funds in three important ways. They have a unique legal status that protects them from bankruptcy. They provide a 10-year guarantee of principal. And they provide a guaranteed death benefit. All three features add value to the product, and therefore justify higher management expense ratios. Indeed, the basic question is: How much more should you be willing to pay in exchange for this guarantee?

I have argued that, roughly speaking, the death benefit is 100 times more valuable to a retired 80-year-old than it is to a 30-year-old. In addition, I have demonstrated that, on a traditional growth fund with a volatility of 15% per year, the justifiable increase in MER is at least 42 basis points. Therefore, if the insurance company is charging 100 basis points (one percentage point) in addition to the annual MER of the underlying mutual fund with 15% volatility, they are charging two and a half times as much as the principal protection is worth.

A 42-basis-point "surcharge" would cover the expense of providing the 10-year guarantee. The higher the volatility of the Seg fund, the more valuable the guarantee to the holder, and the higher the justifiable increase in MER. The lower the volatility, the lower the value of the guarantee — and the lower the justifiable surcharge.

Again, let me reiterate that if you are 80 years old and/or are (unfortunately) on the verge of bankruptcy, the protection is worth much more than the 42 basis points (or 42 cents on one hundred dollars), owing to the shorter expected time horizon. In fact, according to Statistics Canada, an estimated 6,000 to 8,000 people declare personal bankruptcy each month in Canada, so this aspect of the Seg fund is very important, though difficult to value.

Personally, I would recommend these segregated mutual

funds to older investors, perhaps even retirees, and to small business owners seriously concerned with the possibility of bankruptcy. To both types of investor, they are probably a bargain. In practice, I would venture to guess that the young are subsidizing the old. Of course, that assumes that the underlying mutual fund is worth the typical MER of 100 to 200 basis points to begin with. And that is a very big assumption.

Although I have not focused on it here, your first concern in selecting any mutual fund, including a Seg fund, is the likelihood of performance persistence or stability. It would be disastrous to choose a Seg fund based on the lowest MER, only to find that it has the worst performance.

Finally, as with any insurance decision, you must ask yourself two things: How much protection do I need? And am I getting a fair price? The above discussion addresses the latter. Only you, however, can determine the former.

International Diversification: When and Why Does It Make Sense?

The famous economist John Maynard Keynes was once quoted as saying that he did not believe in diversifying his investments — he felt that you should simply buy a few good stocks, and just hold on to them. In stark contrast, Peter Lynch (the legendary Fidelity Investments guru) is rumoured at one point to have owned more than 1,000 different stocks in his mutual fund portfolio.

Keynes's comments aside (how *do* you find those few good stocks?), it's pretty much accepted wisdom that diversifying your investments makes good strategic business sense. "Don't put all your eggs in one basket" was a philosophy preached long before the emergence of modern portfolio theory. In fact, the Babylonian Talmud, compiled more than 2,000 years ago, recommends that a person split his or her wealth into three parts. One-third should be placed in real estate, one-third in money, and the remaining third in business assets, which I liberally interpret to include equities. Overall, not bad investment advice, especially if you could have followed it for the last 2,000 years.

But in all seriousness, why does diversification work? After all, wouldn't you think that the more stocks you own, the more likely you are to catch a loser? Or at least that you're as likely to catch a loser as you are to bag a winner? Is it possible to be over-diversified and own too many stocks? And if it *is* possible, wouldn't these same general issues apply to mutual funds as well? There are now more than 1,500 such funds available in Canada. Does any one mutual fund have enough stocks in them to be labelled "diversified"? How many mutual funds should you own to be properly diversified? The larger question is, how much international exposure should your investments have? Is the current 20% limit that Revenue Canada places on your RRSP assets too severe a restriction?

To answer these and related questions on the benefits of diversification, I would like to present a slightly different perspective. More specifically, I want to focus on the core reasons for diversifying. And I want to do that, as you might have guessed by now, by examining the odds.

Before I get started, however, there's one thing that I should make clear about the whole subject of diversification. There is nothing inherently magical about splitting your money into many small parts and putting each part into a different investment vehicle. The process of splitting the money, or placing it into different mutual funds, is not what's providing the benefit.

Rather, it's the simultaneous movement of these investments that's important. In other words, how do they behave, move, and grow over time? Do they move in lockstep? If one zigs, does the other zag? Obviously, that's an important question, because if the various investments all move in the same direction at the same time, you're not likely to benefit very much from diversifying. In such circumstances, in fact, you might as well pick one good fund, or stock for that matter, and stick with it.

The key — and the secret — to successful diversification is an old axiom: opposites attract.

In investment terms, that means you want to diversify into sectors of the global and local economy that do not share the same up and down influences. For example, if you invest in both the financial services sector and the consumer products sector, you hope that when one is faltering, the other is not. Or if you further diversify into oil and gas and other resource industries, then ideally, if the first two sectors suffer, the third will prosper. The way to quantify, or measure, this parallel movement, is by using something statisticians label a *correlation coefficient*. This coefficient can range from *negative* 100% up to *positive* 100%. The language can be a bit technical, so let me explain how the correlation coefficient works, and why it is so fundamental to the investment process and diversification issues.

First, some generalities. Let's consider two national stock markets — Canada and the U.S., for example. If you think about it for a moment, you'll see that there are three broad possibilities for how these two markets might move vis-à-vis one another, or behave over time. There's a positive correlation, a negative correlation, and no correlation.

The first possibility, the *positive* correlation, simply means or implies that both markets move together in roughly the same average direction. When Canadian stock markets are having a relatively strong week, month, or year, then U.S. markets are doing the same. And when Canadian markets are experiencing difficult times, so are the U.S. markets. Again, this behaviour is said to be positively correlated because both markets move in the same general direction at the same general time. They share the same ups and the same downs. The stronger (or closer) this parallel or co-movement is, the higher the correlation coefficient. In fact, if the two markets moved in perfect lockstep, a statistician would say that they have a correlation coefficient of 100%.

On the other side, we have *negative* correlation. This would mean, for example, that when one market does better than average, the other performs worse than average. When one market has a relatively good week, month, or year, the other has a relatively bad week, month, or year. In the extreme, a correlation coefficient of minus 100% implies that the markets' move in exactly opposite relative directions.

Of course, in the new global economy, it's tough to find such negatively correlated markets. Indeed, more typically, a rising tide lifts all ships (and vice versa). But if you look hard enough, you should be able to find *some* market segments that are counter-cyclical to others. I will return to this subject later in this chapter.

Now, just to get a clearer sense of how this correlation thing operates, here are some numbers. For example, over the last 20 years, the correlation between Canadian equity returns and Canadian long-term government bond returns has been roughly 30%. This — among other things — means that when the Canadian stock market is having a better-than-average month, the Canadian bond market is also having a better-than-average month.

Reviewing the last two decades, statisticians have measured the strength of this positive parallel movement on a scale of 1 to 100 and come up with the number 30. This is definitely a positive correlation coefficient, but not necessarily a *very strong* correlation. Still, it makes a certain amount of intuitive sense that stock and bond markets should move at least partially in tandem, since when interest rates decline, this is good news for both bonds and stocks. Likewise, when interest rates rise, it hurts both markets.

But interest rates are not the only variable that moves stock markets; corporate earnings are even more important. So obviously, the correlation between stock markets and government bond markets (which are not affected by corporate earnings) is nowhere near a perfect 100%.

We might also consider the correlation between returns on gold bullion and Canadian equity markets. In recent decades, the correlation between these two variables has been roughly 15%. In other words, when one index is having a better-than-average month, the other is having a better-than-average month as well. Again, the strength of this positive association is not perfect; many other factors also determine the movement of gold bullion and equity prices. But on a scale of 0% to 100%, these two markets tend to move in the same general direction and share about 15% of the relative ups and downs. Why? For the simple reason that Canadian stock markets are burdened with a disproportionate number of natural resource companies. So when prices for resources — gold, zinc, oil, etc. — are not doing very well, Canadian markets are likely to suffer, and vice versa. Of course, a 15% correlation isn't that strong — and many other industries are represented on the major Canadian exchanges.

So why am I so preoccupied with co-movements and correlations? Who cares if or how different markets move together? Well, as I suggested earlier, correlation is the key and secret to diversification's success.

Think of it this way. Suppose you are faced with two decent investment opportunities. You expect both to make you a few dollars. Moreover, there is a significant additional benefit: the two markets in which you might invest are not perfectly correlated. They do not move together in a parallel direction. Thus, you have a better chance to gain by holding both of them. Let me explain why.

Imagine you split your money equally across the two investments. For various hypothetical correlation scenarios, Table 4.1 shows the probability that you will earn *less* than you would if you invested instead in a one-year 5% GIC.

Table 4.1*

Probability of Falling Short of a One-Year 5% GIC	
Correlation Between Investments	Probability of Shortfall
100%	36.94%
75%	35.33%
50%	33.43%
25%	31.11%
0%	28.18%
−25%	24.28%
−50%	18.63%
−75%	9.44%
−100%	0.00%

*Note: The numbers in this table were calculated by generating thousands of computer-simulated scenarios representing the various correlation levels. In all cases, it was assumed that both investments grow at an annual rate of 15%, with a standard deviation or volatility range of 30%. The probability of shortfall comes from the number of times the return was less than 5% for each of the correlation levels. See Chapters 8 and 9 for more on the computer-simulation methodology.

As you can see, in the most extreme case, when the correlation between the two investments is a perfect 100%, the probability of earning less than the GIC is roughly 37% — very high, indeed. If you knew beforehand that there was almost a two-in-five chance that your investment would fare no better than what you could get from a very secure GIC at your neighbourhood bank, you'd think twice, wouldn't you?

So it seems that with a perfect, 100% correlation, there are absolutely no benefits to diversification. If you split your money into two baskets — but the two baskets are in exactly the same place (two markets that are perfectly correlated) — you have basically kept your eggs in the same basket. By analogy, then, if you diversify into a perfectly correlated investment, the odds of earning less than a standard 5% GIC are the same as if you did not diversify — and simply kept all your money in the one original investment.

At the other extreme is the correlation coefficient of *negative* 100%. In this case, if you split your money between two investments, the odds of earning less than a GIC are reduced to a perfect zero. In other words, you will *never do worse* than the GIC. You will always beat the GIC's 5%. You have basically taken two risky investments, put them together in your investment portfolio, and created a situation in which you will never lose money. Not bad at all.

Wait a minute, you might be saying. What's the catch? How can he guarantee that I won't lose money?

Well, of course I can't. Remember, this is purely a hypothetical example in which the correlation coefficient is artificially set to minus 100%. In practice, you can never really find such a situation. Think again about the example. If one investment does better than average by x%, when the other performs worse than average by x%, then the good return more or less nullifies the bad return, and you are left with the average. In sum, the perfect negative correlation means that any bad surprises from one investment will be offset with good surprises from the other asset. Put them both together in the same portfolio, and you have no surprises.

Now, you may be thinking that if the two investments are perfectly correlated in a negative fashion, why don't they completely cancel each other out, leaving you nothing at the end of the year? If one completely zigs, when the other completely zags, shouldn't you be left with a flat profile?

Not exactly. Remember that negative (or positive) correlations are rarely 100%. More importantly, I did not say that when one investment goes up 8%, the other goes down 8%. I said that when one goes *up* by more than the average performance of the market, the other goes *down* by more than the average performance of the market.

Both investments, however, are expected to increase — in Table 4.1, I assumed by 15% per year. The perfect negative correlation therefore means that when one market goes up 23% (8% more than the 15% average expected), the other will increase by only 7% (8% less than the 15% average expected). In other words, one has climbed 8% more than average, while the other has risen 8% less than average. But both have gone up.

Enough with perfect correlations. Let's take a look at the more reasonable and more common middle ground. In other words, let's see what happens when you diversify into investments that have correlations that are much greater than *negative* 100% and much smaller than *positive* 100%. For example, in Table 4.1, you will see that if the correlation coefficient is exactly zero — i.e., there is absolutely no relationship between the two investments' movements — the probability of earning less than a 5% GIC is roughly 28%. Compare that with the 37% chance of doing worse than the GIC on each individual investment, or by having all your eggs in the same or one basket.

This is a reduction of 37% – 28% = 9%. In short, by splitting your money into two parts, you are reducing considerably the risk of underperforming the GIC. Thus, as you can see, even though the correlation between the two investments is zero — i.e., if one does better than average, there is no indication of how the other will perform — there are still benefits to diversifying.

Similarly, if the correlation coefficient is *negative* 25%, the odds of your portfolio doing worse than the GIC is 24% (or about one in four). Compare that with the 28% chance of doing worse when the correlation is zero. Once again, the benefits are clear. The lower the correlation between the two investments, the lower your risk.

I like to call this the fundamental law of diversification: "The risk of the sum is less than the sum of the risk."

What do I mean? Remember that you need two ingredients or factors for successful diversification. The first is non-perfect correlation; the second is an expectation of some profit from both investments. How much you benefit from diversification will depend on the strength of these two factors.

By adding two imperfectly correlated assets, you are reducing the shortfall risk compared to the individual shortfall risks of each asset. The risk of the sum — i.e., the risk of the portfolio that consists of two assets — is less than the sum of the risks — i.e., just adding the risk of each individual asset.

Let me clarify this point by walking through a detailed example. We know that if you put $100 in a GIC that pays 5% per annum, you'll have $105 at the end of the year. Now, let's say you want to invest, take some risk, and diversify. Instead of buying the GIC, you put $50 in one asset (let's call it Fund XYZ), and $50 in another (Fund ABC).

Now, we know from Table 4.1 that if there is zero correlation between the price movements of these two investments, then you stand a 28% chance of having less than $105 at the end of the year. This is what I call the *risk of the sum*. It's the risk of your capital, or the risk of your portfolio.

On the other hand, if you put the entire $100 in any one asset, either Fund XYZ or Fund ABC, the chance of earning less than $105 now rises to 37%. This is what I call the *sum of the risk*. The fundamental law of diversification in action means that the risk of the sum (28%) is less than the sum of the risk (37%).

An additional point to mention is that in Table 4.1, we are dealing with a one-year horizon. It examines the shortfall odds over a 12-month period. So what happens if we extend this correlation analysis to a longer time horizon?

Table 4.2 paints the longer-term picture. This time the returns on money split equally between two investments (in various correlation scenarios) are compared at five years (with a five-year 5% compounded GIC) and at 10 years (with a hypothetical 10-year 5% GIC).

Table 4.2*

Probability of Falling Short of 5- and 10-Year GICs		
Correlation Between Investments	5-Year Probability of Shortfall	10-Year Probability of Shortfall
100%	22.80%	14.59%
75%	20.00%	11.70%
50%	16.92%	8.79%
25%	13.53%	5.96%
0%	9.83%	3.39%
−25%	5.94%	1.37%
−50%	2.31%	0.24%
−75%	0.17%	0.00%
−100%	0.00%	0.00%

*Note: Both investments are expected to grow at an annual rate of 15%, with a standard deviation or volatility range of 30%. The probability that each individual asset will earn less than 5% compounded for five years is exactly 22.80%; for 10 years it is 14.59%.

As you can see, Table 4.2 has uniformly lower shortfall probabilities than those in Table 4.1. What does that mean? It means that the odds of earning less than a five-year compounded 5% GIC decrease the longer you hold the investment. This concept was introduced in the Introduction, when I discussed the effect of time horizons on shortfall risk. As I argued then, the longer you hold an investment, the lower the probability of regret.

But even more important than the time-horizon effect in Table 4.2 is the fact that the amount by which the shortfall risk is reduced depends on the correlation coefficient between the two assets that you are mixing in your portfolio. In other words, the lower the correlation, the lower the risk.

Compare, for example, the zero correlation case. In Table 4.1 — looking at risk over a one-year period — the probability of shortfall was roughly 28%. But in the case of a five-year horizon with zero correlation between the assets, the probability of shortfall is reduced to roughly 10%. Over 10 years, the same zero correlation between the two investments leads to a shortfall risk of approximately 3%. Isn't it remarkable what four — or nine — more years of investing can do?

The reduction is even more pronounced if you look at a *negative* 50% correlation. Remember, a negative correlation means that when one asset is doing *better* than average, the other is doing *worse* than average. In other words, they are generally moving in the opposite relative direction. The *negative* 50% is midpoint on a scale of negative 100% to 0%, and measures the relative strength of this opposite movement. In Table 4.1, the one-year horizon case, the probability of shortfall is roughly 19%. In Table 4.2, the five-year horizon, the odds are reduced to a mere 2%. For 10 years, it is reduced to less than a quarter of a percentage point. Notice the effect of time — and the effect of correlation.

What, then, are the lessons?

Two things will reduce the shortfall risk of your portfolio: (1) the longer time horizon over which you hold the portfolio; and (2) the movement of the assets in your portfolio.

The more independently they move — i.e., the lower their correlation — the more your risk is reduced.

I like to argue that there are two dimensions to investment diversification — time and space. (No, I have not been watching too many *Star Trek* episodes.) By *time*, I mean the length of time you hold the portfolio; the longer you hold it, the more diversified your portfolio becomes. If you consider the essence of diversification to be the reduction of shortfall risk — because of the imperfect correlation — then holding the portfolio for longer periods of time will also reduce shortfall risk.

I believe that when you invest in Canadian equities during the year of 1998 and during the year of 1999, you are essentially holding two different investments. Sure, they are the same asset class — namely, Canadian equities. But the returns from these two investments are most likely uncorrelated; that is, the return in one year is independent of the return in the next. If Canadian equities do better than average during 1998, the odds are still only 50/50 that they'll do better than average during 1999. So I would argue

Table 4.3*

Space/Time Diversification: Probability of Falling Short of a 5% Compounded GIC

Space (Portfolio Contents)	Time (Holding Period)				
	1 year	5 years	10 years	15 years	20 years
1 fund	36.94%	22.80%	14.59%	9.84%	6.80%
2 funds	28.18%	9.83%	3.39%	1.27%	0.49%
3 funds	22.65%	4.66%	0.88%	0.18%	0.04%
4 funds	18.63%	2.31%	0.24%	0.03%	0.00%
5 funds	15.54%	1.17%	0.07%	0.00%	0.00%

Note: Each and every mutual fund is expected to grow at an annual rate of 15%, with a standard deviation or volatility range of 30%. The correlation coefficient is assumed to be zero between all assets.

that you diversify your investments by holding both — equities in 1998 and equities in 1999. You see, in my opinion, the word "diversification" is not just about diversity at any one point in time; it's actually about investing in products that do not move together, so that your shortfall risk (probability of regret) is reduced. Therefore, investing for long periods of time in one asset is qualitatively similar to investing in different assets over one period of time.

By *space* diversification, I mean that the more independent assets you have in your portfolio (independent in the sense of not moving in tandem with each other), the more diversified the portfolio becomes. I chose the word "space" to reflect this principle because when you diversify across geographic and economic boundaries, you are likely — though not necessarily guaranteed — to find investment assets that move independently.

Here is how you would read Table 4.3. For example, if you split your money equally across three independent (i.e., zero-correlated) mutual fund investments — and hold this portfolio for five years — the odds of doing worse than a 5% compounded GIC are precisely 4.66%. This is a 4.66% chance of regret. In other words, there is a 100% – 4.66% = 95.44% chance of doing better than the GIC.

Likewise, if you split your money equally across five independent (zero-correlated) mutual fund investments — and hold this portfolio for 10 years — there is a 0.07% (seven in 1,000) chance that you will earn less than the 5% GIC. This reduction — across space and time — is a manifestation of investment diversification.

Notice that as you move down and to the right — i.e., as you increase the number of funds and the holding period — the shortfall risk declines. In fact, this limited table is just a small view of the bigger picture. If you added more time and more independent assets, you would continue to reduce the risk.

But please remember the crucial operating assumption in Table 4.3 — the independent or zero correlation between the funds. If the correlation between the funds is greater than zero, that is, if they move to some extent in the same general direction, the shortfall probability will not be as low because the space diversification effect will not be as strong. The exact numbers, of course, would depend on the precise correlation structure of the mutual funds involved.

In summary, Figure 4.1 provides a graphic illustration of the effects of both space (the number of funds) and time (the number of years) on the probability of shortfall.

I readily concede that things begin to get a bit theoretical with some of these assumptions. Still, I do hope you grasp the main point that emerges from this general approach — namely, the positive effect of more time (a longer holding period) and more space (more investments that move independently of each other) on your portfolio. Now let me address some of the real-world issues.

Practically speaking, if your investment portfolio is holding only Canadian, broad-based equity investments, you are subjecting yourself — in one year — to a 37% risk of not beating a GIC that pays 5%. This conclusion comes from Table 4.3's one-year, one-fund case. In any one year, there's almost a 40% chance that you will earn less than the 5% GIC. But — and here is the crux — if you can find and invest in another asset class, which is expected to increase, but is not perfectly correlated with your first, Canadian-based equity investment, you will gain from the law of diversification. And the less correlated this asset class, mutual fund, or investment is with the Canadian market, the greater will be your gain.

Historically, for example, the U.S. market has had a 60% positive correlation with the Canadian market and is expected to increase in the long run. Hence, both ingredients for successful diversification are present. Therefore,

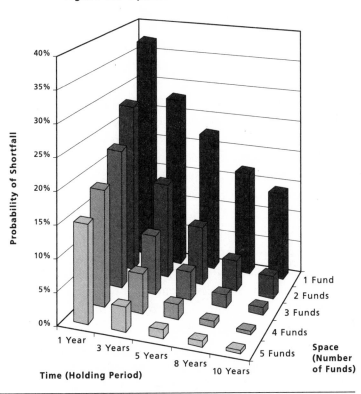

Figure 4.1 Space/Time Diversification

you should and will be able to reduce your shortfall risk by diversifying part of your investments into the U.S. market. In other words, your odds of doing worse than a safe 5% GIC will decrease if you diversify your investments into the United States, because the correlation between the two markets is less than 100%.

In fact, there really is nothing special about the U.S. market. The correlation between the Canadian stock market and the German stock market, for instance, is roughly 40%. This correlation is even lower than the one with the U.S., which according to Table 4.1 implies that — everything else being equal — diversifying into Germany would reduce your shortfall risk even more than diversifying into the United States. This does not mean you should avoid the U.S. in favour of Germany; there is room in your portfolio for both the U.S. and German markets. As you can see from Table 4.3, the more funds, the merrier.

Similarly, there is nothing special or extraordinary about German stocks. In fact, Italy (a 30% correlation), the United Kingdom (a 50% correlation), and Switzerland (a 55% correlation) also have stock markets that are not perfectly correlated with the Canadian market. Presumably, you would also benefit from diversifying into those markets.

The same diversification principle, of course, is applicable to more than just national stock markets. Bonds, real estate, precious metals, commodities, and even art do not move with perfect correlation to Canadian equity markets. The actual correlations vary over time (more on this topic a bit later), but there is room for most of these asset classes in a well-balanced portfolio because they will all help to reduce your shortfall risk — the risk of doing worse than the risk-free, 5% GIC benchmark. Remember the two ingredients, though. They must have imperfect correlation *and* they must have a reasonable chance of making some money over time. (The price of Elvis memorabilia is not correlated with the general stock markets, but I'm not sure about the growth prospects . . .)

So what, then, is the right amount for you? Precisely how much should you invest in each of these asset classes? What allocation is the right one given your circumstances? How much should you invest in the U.S., the U.K., Germany, or even Japan?

Good questions. Unfortunately, as is often the case with investment decisions, the answers depend on your personal circumstances, needs, requirements, fears, and phobias — otherwise known as your attitude toward risk. I cannot pretend to have a cookie-cutter, formulaic answer that will fit all possible contingencies. In fact, I am very much averse to computer programs and black-box "solutions" to your investment needs. You must discuss these issues with your financial planner, investment adviser, broker, or even tax accountant.

My objectives here are, in that sense, more modest. I want to explain the general framework, to show you the odds, and to argue the benefits of diversification. I hope I've given you the information you need to ask intelligent questions and appreciate the underlying issues.

In that light, let me now turn to the following caveats. In some ways, they may be more important than the previous pages of this chapter.

CONCLUSION

Although in this chapter — and in most of this book, for that matter — I focus on shortfall risk as the intuitive measure of financial uncertainty, there are many other acceptable and useful ways to approach, quantify, and measure risk. A shortfall risk of 10%, for example, implies that in one out of every 10 attempts, you will do worse than a risk-free GIC. But how much worse will you do? How bad can it get in any one year or in any one quarter? Some shortfalls are worse than other shortfalls. Many investors certainly experienced one hell of a shortfall in the third quarter of 1998. So, once again, when making your own financial decisions, make sure to inquire: How bad can it get? And what are the odds of it getting that bad?

Nevertheless, the concept of correlation is the single most important variable in determining the success of national and international diversification. The law of diversification states that the risk of the sum is less than the sum of the risk. The lower the correlation between the investments in your portfolio, the greater the benefit of diversification.

But what if, instead of investing in mutual funds, you decided to build your own investment portfolio? Many investors do. In that case, you'd always be on the lookout for investments that moved up in the long run, but that did not necessarily move together. As Tables 4.1 and 4.2 indicate, the lower the correlation, the lower your portfolio risk will be.

In general, most Canadian stocks tend to move together; that is, their correlation coefficient is quite high. That means you must hold more than just a few stocks to benefit from the law of diversification. I would argue — based on the methodology introduced in Table 4.3 — that you would need at least 25 to 30 individual stocks, drawn from different sectors of the economy, to fully benefit from the diversification effect. Anything less than that, I submit, would leave you with undesirable shortfall risk.

Furthermore, with the correlation coefficient between the world at large and Canadian equity markets in the 50% region, Table 4.2 shows the undeniable effect of international diversification. Over a 10-year period, if you placed half of your investments in a portfolio of stocks from the world at large and half in Canada, you would reduce your shortfall risk from 15% to 9% — even if all markets were expected to appreciate at the same rate! Therefore, aside from the higher relative returns that international markets have experienced over the last few years, the pure risk reduction is another excellent argument for relaxing the foreign-content restrictions on registered pension plans.

In other words, the reason to invest internationally is not simply because those markets have done better in the past — who's to say that performance will continue? The main — and perhaps more subtle — reason is the shortfall reduction that takes place when you diversify into imperfectly correlated investments.

Unfortunately, the problem with correlation is that it

seems to break down when you need it most. In the good old 1970s and 1980s, you could find international stock markets that moved independently or with relatively low correlation. Lately, this doesn't seem to be the case. In fact, in recent good times, different markets have tended to obey their historic correlation with each other. In other words, they co-move by the right or expected amount. In bad times, however, when world markets are suffering, everybody and everything seems to go down at exactly the same time. In a climate of stress or investment shocks, correlation coefficients tend to move toward 100%. This means, for example, that when North American markets zag, the rest of the world zags even more. This disturbing reality was best illustrated during the third quarter of 1998, when virtually every international equity market was decimated.

So what, in the end, does that tell us about the benefits of diversification? Well, in my opinion, the practical concept of diversification is not as powerful as theory would suggest. In fact, as international capital markets become increasingly integrated, as capital flows are liberated and national regulations are reduced, the odds are that correlations will increase. No longer will the financial economies of Europe, North America, and the Far East march to different drummers.

Federal tax authorities may eventually decide to liberalize the foreign-content restrictions in RRSP and pension plans. By then, however, it may be too late.

What's So Wonderful About Index-Linked GICs?

In the 1990s, a new investment vehicle appeared in Canada. It was known formally as an index-linked (or equity-linked) Guaranteed Investment Certificate, with the somewhat awkward acronym ILGIC.

Since making their appearance on the investment scene, these instruments have acquired a certain popularity. My objective here is to determine whether that popularity is deserved, by reviewing what these products are, why they have become so popular, and who sells them (and in what "flavours").

What exactly is an index-linked GIC?

At first glance, the ILGIC is a simple combination of a regular Guaranteed Investment Certificate (GIC) and an equity-based mutual fund. Like the conventional GIC, the index-linked version can be purchased at almost any Canadian bank, credit union, or trust company by committing (read: investing) a certain amount of money for a fixed period of time. Your funds will then be locked up until the chosen maturity date. (There are no "cashable" index-linked GICs.)

Similarly, your original principal investment in an index-linked GIC is guaranteed to be returned at maturity and is insured by federal and provincial deposit corporations. So even in a worst-case scenario, you will always get your money back when the index-linked GIC matures.

But here, alas, is where the similarity ends. With a regular GIC, the interest you earn is determined and agreed upon in advance. It does not change over the life of the certificate. There will be no investment surprises, positive or negative.

For example, let's say that on January 15, 1999, you invested $10,000 in an ordinary two-year (compounding) GIC paying 4% per annum. This means that on January 15, 2001, you will receive your original $10,000 principal, together with $816; that corresponds to the 4% interest rate, compounded for two years.

If this were a non-compounding GIC, your account would be credited with two separate payments of $400 on January 15, 2000, and January 15, 2001.

The net return may seem small. It may even *be* small, relative to other possible investments. But the important thing — and the defining feature of a conventional GIC — is that you know right from the start exactly "what you're going to get."

In rather sharp contrast, with an indexed-linked GIC, you do not know "what you're going to get" until the date of maturity. The interest rate will be determined only when the contract expires. Moreover, the actual interest rate will depend in part on how the stock market index performs —

hence the name, "index-linked." The higher the stock market index goes during the life of your ILGIC, the higher will be your return.

But what if the stock market idles in neutral over the life of your certificate? Worse, what if it crashes? In that case, your investment will earn zero interest. That's the bad news.

The good news is that your original principal is guaranteed. Even if the stock market index were to collapse, the worst that could happen is that you'd get all of your money back at maturity.

Now, the actual relationship between the performance of the stock market index and the interest rate credited to your account depends on a formula. At times, as you will read later in this chapter, that formula can be quite complicated. The important thing to remember here is that the interest rate payable on index-linked GICs is unknown until the certificate matures. Of course, you can get a pretty good estimate of your probable return by monitoring the overall performance of the stock market index over the life of the index-linked GIC.

There are other complexities to consider as well. Many different types of index-linked GICs are available in Canada. The differences depend on

1. the length or maturity date of the contract;
2. the exact formula used to calculate the interest rate; and
3. the stock market to which the product is linked.

For example, you can buy an index-linked GIC that matures anywhere from two to five years out, and is linked to stock markets in Canada, the United States, Europe, or even the Far East. For investors, the wide variety of products can be confusing and difficult to evaluate. One of the goals of this discussion is to help you clarify this haze.

Let's consider, for instance, a product recently offered by Scotiabank — a two-year index-linked GIC whose rate of return is tied to the performance of the Toronto 35 Composite Value Stock Index over a 24-month time frame. Your investment return will depend on the composite value index of the TSE35 (which excludes any dividends) at maturity.

If you invest a hypothetical $1,000 and the TSE35 decreases over the two-year period, you will receive your original deposit (guaranteed) with no interest earned.

If the TSE35 increases during that time, you will receive the return from the TSE35. In other words, if the index rises by 10%, you will receive $1,100 (the original $1,000 plus 10% interest). If it rises by 20%, you'll earn $1,200 ($1,000 plus 20%).

So what's the catch? Why bother investing in stocks, mutual funds, or anything else for that matter, if you can buy index-linked GICs with no downside risk? The astute reader may already have discovered the answers.

1. The underlying TSE35 index, from which your return is computed, does not include dividends. Whatever dividends may be payable by the 35 stocks that make up the index, during the life of your contract, will not accrue to you.

2. If indeed the market declines, your principal capital will be returned in full at maturity. But in the meantime, you will have lost the potential interest income that could have been obtained from a conventional GIC. Economists refer to this as the "lost opportunity" cost.

3. In many cases, the formula for computing the return on the index-linked GICs is capped at a fixed annual percentage rate. If the underlying index, net of dividends, is greater than the capped rate, you do not participate

in any further upward movement. For example, the Scotiabank product described above has a "growth cap" of 20%; this means that if the TSE35 increased by more than 20%, you would receive 20% at maturity — no more. Any additional increase in the market value of the TSE35 would be lost.

Now, using an investment of $10,000, let's compare the Scotiabank two-year index-linked GIC with an ordinary 4% compounded GIC.

Table 5.1

Return of TSE35	Index-Linked GIC	Regular GIC
Negative	$10,000	$10,816
Between 0% and 20%	$10,000(1 + R)*	$10,816
Greater than 20%	$12,000	$10,816

*If the TSE35 increases by 0%–20%, a number I denote by the letter R in percentage terms, the payoff will be $10,000(1 + R).

Thus, the certainty of the $816 must be weighed against the uncertainty of anything between $0 and $2,000. Historically, the compounded rate of return from the TSE35 — excluding dividends — has been about 6.5% per year. The number 6.5% may seem fairly low, but remember, it doesn't include dividends, which make a big difference.

If you project the 6.5% rate for two years, it would yield an expected payment of $11,342 on the ILGIC — $526 more than the regular GIC. That would make it a pretty good deal, on average. Of course, averages can be very deceiving, and there is no guarantee that history will repeat itself. As I said in the Introduction, you have to look at the probabilities. Indeed, there is a decent chance that you may get more than $11,342 at maturity. But there is also a chance that you will only get your $10,000 back at maturity.

Another helpful way to understand how index-linked GICs work is through a payoff diagram. This is a graphic depiction of the formula that describes the relationship between the performance of the underlying stock market index and the interest rate paid at maturity. The payoff diagram for Scotiabank's index-linked GIC (or any other two-year product with a 20% cap) is illustrated in Figure 5.1.

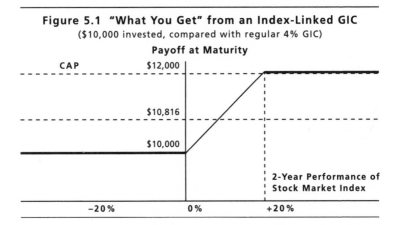

Figure 5.1 "What You Get" from an Index-Linked GIC
($10,000 invested, compared with regular 4% GIC)

As you can see, at maturity, you get your principal back — regardless of how the stock market index performs. The interest you earn, however, will depend on how the stock market does over the two years. If the return (net of dividends) of the underlying index at maturity is zero or negative, you will get no interest at all. If, on the other hand, the return is between 0% and 20%, you will get exactly that percentage. Finally, if the return is greater than 20%, your return is capped at 20%; you will not participate in any further upward movement.

Of course, if this cap were not in place, the payoff line in the above diagram would continue to increase in sync with the underlying index. The cap may seem like a small price to pay for the downside protection, but it's likely to cause some regret if, at maturity, the underlying index exceeds the cap, and you cannot enjoy the benefit.

Furthermore, the caps are usually quoted on a total return

basis, which gives the illusion that they are very high. In fact, on an annualized basis, they tend to be quite low.

Let's examine another product, this time offered by the National Bank of Canada. This is a five-year index-linked GIC, again tied to the TSE35 stock market index. The cap, here, is 60%, which means that if the TSE35 increases by more than 60% over the five-year period, your return will be 60%, no more.

On an annualized basis, this cap works out to 9.8%. From this particular index-linked GIC, 9.8% is the most you will earn annually.

Let me explain. A cap of 60% over a five-year period means that if you start with $100, the absolute maximum you can get back in five years — the best-case scenario — is $160. To get a better feel for this number, and to success-fully compare it with a regular GIC, we should annualize the cap rate. Note that to compute the annualized rate over five years, the 60% should *not* be divided by five (which would yield 12%), because it overestimates the true annual cap by ignoring the compounding effect of interest; instead, it should be factored by five, which will yield the number 9.8%.

(For mathematical purists and keen investment buffs, the correct way to do this is to subtract 1 from the fifth root of 1.6. This is expressed as $(1.6)^{(1/5)} - 1 = 9.8\%$.)

On an annualized basis, then, a 60% five-year cap is equiv-alent to a yield of 9.8% per annum. In other words, if you invest $100 in a compound GIC earning 9.8% per annum for five years, you will get $100 (1.098) (1.098) (1.098) (1.098) (1.098) = 100 (1.098)^5 = \$160$ in five years. Therefore, I argue that the most you can earn, per year, on the above index-linked GIC is 9.8%.

Clearly, if you have the choice, no cap is always better than a cap and, obviously, the higher the cap, the better.

Figure 5.2 "What You Get" from a Regular GIC
Payoff at Maturity

8.16%

2-Year Performance of
Stock Market Index

−20%   0%   +20%

Now, Figure 5.2 is the payoff diagram for a two-year conventional 4% GIC. As you can see, the payoff line is flat; it does not really depend on the performance of the stock market index. No matter what happens to the underlying index, your total return will be 8.16% — or 4% compounded for two years.

Finally, Figure 5.3 shows what might result if you purchased the actual TSE35 composite value index (the index net of dividends). Think of an equity-based mutual fund that moves according to changes in the overall market.

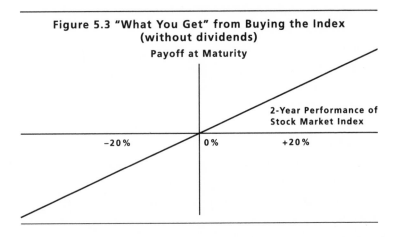

Figure 5.3 "What You Get" from Buying the Index
(without dividends)
Payoff at Maturity

2-Year Performance of
Stock Market Index

−20%   0%   +20%

You will note (to the right of the vertical axis) that Figure 5.3 bears some resemblance to the payoff diagram of an index-linked GIC: what you get moves in lockstep with the underlying market index.

The difference here is that you get to participate fully in any upward tick of the index. There is no cap. Of course, you must take the bad with the good; if the underlying index falls during the holding period, your return will be negative, and you will lose part of your principal. That never happens with index-linked or regular GICs. But practically speaking, you are paying for that downside protection by (a) forfeiting dividends and (b) ceding the right to receive any returns above the cap.

In the lingo of economists, you cannot get something for nothing. If an index-linked GIC product were offered in Canada with no cap and if the underlying market index were based on the total return, including dividends, that indeed would be a free lunch.

Why Are They So Popular?

Stock markets in 1997–98 soared to new, historical (and perhaps hysterical) highs. Concerned that the bull rally could not endure forever, investors naturally went looking for downside protection. That is entirely natural and pre-dictable behaviour. Fear, remember, is as powerful a force in the psychology of markets as greed. Investors who have enjoyed a healthy run-up in prices can be expected to wonder if it isn't time to sell, to take profits and find other, safer havens for their capital. They want protection from a market correction or crash. The recent volatility of the Dow Jones Industrial Average and other indexes suggests that this instinct for preservation is not misplaced.

That, I submit, goes some distance toward explaining why ILGICs have gained as much penetration as they have in the marketplace. They're safe, secure and, like a good cup of cocoa, will help you sleep through the night.

Who Sells Them and in What Flavours?

Table 5.2 summarizes the different products available in Canada. You can purchase index-linked GICs from a bank, trust company, or credit union, and the products themselves differ on four main elements: the term of the contract; the index to which the GIC is linked; the formula used to determine the maturity value of the GIC; and the lock-in feature (or lack thereof).

The Term. ILGICs are available with terms of two, three, four, or five years.

The important thing to remember is that the implicit insurance provided by an index-linked GIC gets cheaper the longer the term of your contract. This is in stark contrast to mainstream insurance, such as car, health, and life, where, as one would expect, the longer the policy is to stay in force, the more it costs to acquire the protection.

The main reason for the reduced cost is that, in the event of a crash (or prolonged market decline), you only get your original money back after the two-, three-, four-, or five-year period ends. You simply cannot reclaim your original investment the day after a market crash.

Therefore, everything else being equal, an index-linked GIC that provides upside market potential, but promises to repay your principal in three years, is more valuable than an index-linked GIC with a five-year maturity.

The Index. The next choice to make when shopping around is which underlying index you want linked to your GIC. Now, this may seem paradoxical, but even though there are large benefits to diversifying internationally, a narrowly based index-linked GIC is more valuable than one that is widely based.

Table 5.2 ILGIC Products Available in Canada

Institution	Underlying Index	Maturity	Cap/Floor (%)	Averaging	Participation Factor*	In & out of RSP?	Lock-in Ability	Minimum Investment
Bank of Montreal	TSE35 SP500 G7 index[1]	3 or 5 years	60/0	Last 6 months	Varies	Yes	No	$1,000
Royal Bank	TSE35 Global[2]	3 or 5 years	No cap/0	Last 12 months	Varies	Yes	Yes	$1,000
	5-in-1 GIC TSE35	5 years: 20% redeemed/year	20/0	No	Varies	Yes	No	$5,000
Scotiabank	TSE35 G7 index[3]	2 years 3 years	20/0 30/0	No	100%	Yes	No	$500
Toronto Dominion	TSE100 SP500 Global[4]	3 or 5 years	No cap/0	Last 12 months	Varies	Yes	No	$500 for RSP $1,000 otherwise
CIBC	TSE35	3 or 5 years	No cap/0	Last 12 months	Varies	Yes	No	$500
	Market Mix[5]	3 or 5 years	No cap/0	Last 12 months	Varies	Yes	No	$500
National Bank	TSE35	2 or 5 years	2-year: 16.8/0 5-year: 70/0	Last 4 months	100%	Yes	No	$500
Canada Trust	TSE100 World Market[6]	3 or 5 years	3-year: 25/0 5-year: No cap/0	Last 12 months	100%	Self-directed RSP only	No	$1,000 $500
Manulife Bank	TSE35 G-7[7]	5 years	No cap/0	Last 12 months	100%	Yes	No	$5,000
Citizens Bank	TSE35[8]	5 years	No cap/0	No	100%	Yes	No	$1,000
HongKong Bank	TSE35 Hang Seng 33 G7[9]	3 years	40/0	Last 12 months	100%	Yes	No	$1,000

Table 5.2 (continued)

Institution	Underlying Index	Maturity	Cap/Floor (%)	Averaging	Participation Factor*	In & out of RSP?	Lock-in Ability	Minimum Investment
Trimark Trust	TSE35[10]	3 years	35/0	Last 12 months	50%	Yes	After each year	$1,000
London Life	TSE35	38 months	60/1	Monthly averages	100%	Yes	No	$1,000
MRS Trust	TSE35	3 or 5 years	No cap/0	Last 12 months	Varies	Yes	No	$500
	G7[11]							
Sun Life Trust	TSE35	5 years	No cap/0	No	100%	Yes	No	$1,000
	MSCI			Annual averages				
Hepcoe Credit Union	TSE35		No cap/0	Monthly averages	150%	Yes	No	$100 for RSP
	SP500	5 years	No cap/0	Quarterly averages	120%	Yes	After each year	$1,000 otherwise
Metro Credit Union	TSE35	3 or 5 years	No cap/0	Monthly averages	100%	Yes	No	$500
DUCA	TSE35	3 or 5 years	No cap/0	Monthly averages	3-year: 100% 5-year: 150%	Yes	No	$2,000

Notes to Table 5.2

* When the participation factors vary, they are determined at the beginning of the contract and are then in effect for the duration of the term.
1 25% TSE35, 25% SP500, 10% in each of: FTSE100, CAC40, DAX30, Nikkei 225, MIB30
2 20% in each of the following: CAC40, DAX30, FTSE100, Nikkei 225, SP500
3 25% SP500, 20% Nikkei 225, 15% DAX30, 15% CAC40, 10% FTSE100, 10% TSE35, 5% MIB30
4 30% TSE100, 20% SP500, 20% FTSE100, 10% Nikkei 225, 10% DAX30, 5% CAC40, 5% MIB30
5 Depending on purchaser's risk profile, there are six different products that can be selected. They vary in their weightings of the following: CIBC Wood Gundy Government of Canada Bond Index, TSE35, Nikkei 225, FTSE Eurotop 100, SP500, and regular fixed return GICs.
6 25% SP500, 25% Nikkei 225, 15% TSE35, 10% FTSE100, 5% in each of: CAC40, AEX, DAX, Australia, and Switzerland
7 30% SP500, 20% Nikkei 225, 15% TSE35, 15% MIB30, 10% in each of: FTSE100, DAX30, CAC40
8 The companies in the TSE35 are ethically screened. Currently, the GIC measures the performance of 22 of the 35 companies.
9 40% SP500, 20% Nikkei 225, 10% in each of: FTSE100, DAX30, CAC40; 5% in each of: TSE35, MIB30
10 The GIC's return is based 50% on the performance of the TSE35 and 50% on the Scotia McLeod Universal Bond Fund.
11 20% SP500, 20% Nikkei 225, 15% FTSE100, 15% DAX30, 10% in each of: TSE35, CAC40, MIB30

You might ask: How can that be? Isn't it common knowledge that investment diversification increases portfolio value? Isn't it true that a diversified portfolio of stocks mitigates and reduces overall volatility?

Why, then, would I say that a GIC linked to a narrow, undiversified, and volatile index is more valuable?

The key is the volatility.

Think of it this way. Let's say an insurance agent offered you a car insurance policy with absolutely no deductible for $1,000 per year, on any car of your choice. Which car would you insure — the cheapest or the most expensive? Or would it really matter?

Naturally, for the same $1,000, I would insure my most expensive car. The insurance is more valuable to me when the potential damage is higher.

Or, stated differently, let's say the same insurance agent offered you a policy with absolutely no deductible for $1,000 per year, covering any one member of your family. Who would you insure — your 19-year-old daughter, Natalie, with a perfect driving record, or your 17-year-old son Jonathan, with three fender-benders already on his new licence?

Clearly, you'd put your son on the policy and get other insurance for your daughter. Why? Because you'd get the best value for your $1,000 insurance by covering the most volatile and risky item that you could insure.

The same thinking applies to ILGICs, because you are buying insurance coverage on the same $100 initial investment. Which index would you rather link to — the most volatile or the most stable? I would go with the most volatility, which gives me the highest value for my insurance dollar. Consequently, since the narrow index is the most volatile, I would pick the narrowest of indices, which is normally associated with the highest volatility.

Similarly, if your initial investment sum is $7,000, it

would be preferable to buy seven $1,000 GICs, each linked to one of seven national indices, than to buy a single $7,000 GIC linked to an index of seven countries.

In other words, for the same price, would you rather purchase insurance covering both Natalie and Jonathan with one cumulative damage deductible of $500, or two separate policies with a deductible of $250 per policy? I would go with a $250 deductible per child.

Let's not confuse the *need* for insurance with the *value* of insurance. If your investment portfolio is heavily weighted toward Canadian common and preferred shares, you should welcome the opportunity to link your investment returns to a broader international index. In that regard, a broad-based index-linked GIC is better than a narrow one. But in terms of value, the question is, which one provides the greatest value per dollar invested? Clearly the narrow one.

Remember, for the same price, insure the reckless driver in the priciest car, even though you don't really want Jonathan driving your Lexus.

Once these choices are made, there is very little flexibility; the other decisions, such as the averaging period, the minimum interest paid, and the caps are determined by the institution selling the product.

The Formula. The formula is an algebraic relationship that illustrates the connection between the underlying market index and what you earn at maturity. But you don't need to understand mathematical symbols to display a formula. Here is our earlier example; pay particular attention to the boldface expressions, which represent the formula:

If the TSE35 decreases, you receive the original deposit. This can be expressed as follows:

Market < 0% implies Return = 0%

If the TSE35 increases, but by less than 20%, you receive the total return from the TSE35.

0% < Market < 20% implies 0% < Return < 20%

If, on the other hand, the TSE35 increases by more than 20%, you receive the maximum 20% at maturity.

Market > 20% implies Return = 20%

In some cases, the relationship between the underlying market index and the payoff from an index-linked GIC is not as straightforward as the above. Some products contain an averaging and participation feature, which tends to reduce your return.

In the past, the Bank of Montreal offered a five-year index-linked GIC tied to the TSE300 index, with no cap. However, the formula depended on the monthly closing price of the TSE300 composite value index (net of dividends, as usual). The formula added up the 60 monthly closing prices over the five years, and then divided by 60 to obtain a value for the return. (There was also a minimal guaranteed interest rate.)

In my judgment, this type of index-linked GIC is opaque and frustrating for consumers. That's because it's extremely difficult to determine how you are doing over the life of the product. Furthermore, the process of averaging tends to reduce the overall payoff from the index-linked GIC. Why is this so?

Let's assume that averaging takes place annually, instead of monthly, for the five-year period. Imagine you bought the ILGIC on January 1, 1998, so it would mature on January 1, 2003. Let's also assume a fictitious set of closing (settlement) numbers for the underlying index over the five years.

Base (Purchasing) Date:	Dec. 31, 1997	Closed at: 6,000
Measurement Date #1	Dec. 31, 1998	Closed at: 6,500
Measurement Date #2	Dec. 31, 1999	Closed at: 7,000
Measurement Date #3	Dec. 31, 2000	Closed at: 7,500
Measurement Date #4	Dec. 31, 2001	Closed at: 8,000
Measurement Date #5	Dec. 31, 2002	Closed at: 8,500

Note that the index has increased from 6,000 to 8,500, on the last measurement date (December 31, 2002). This represents a yield of about 42%, which is an average of approximately 7.3% per year, for each of the five years compounded. Hence, an investment of $100 would produce $142 after five years. In other words, an ILGIC with no averaging provision and no cap invested in this index would pay $142 for every $100 invested.

Now, let's examine the effect of averaging.

This Bank of Montreal–type product (available also from many credit unions) would calculate the interest rate on the ILGIC based on the average of the five year-end prices. Specifically, the formula would take the average of 6,500, 7,000, 7,500, 8,000, 8,500 — exactly 7,500 — and then assume that 7,500 is the final value of the index. It would then divide the average (7,500) by the base level (6,000). The result, 1.25, means that your investment would yield a 25% gain. In plain English, the final payoff on an ILGIC with this type of averaging feature and stock market scenario would be $125 for every $100 invested, even though the index itself actually increased by 42%.

Thus, for every $100 invested, averaging means you lose $17. For a $1,000 contract, you'd lose $170. These are not insignificant amounts.

The rationale of averaging may be quite honourable — namely, to reduce the volatility of the final payoff. But it ends up reducing the actual payoff and value of the index-linked GIC.

Now, some readers may find this argument difficult to accept. They may posit a different scenario, in which the stock market collapses during the year 2002 and the index falls back to its base level (6,000) by December 31.

In this case, the standard non-averaged ILGIC would pay nothing, of course, since the index ended where it began, going from 6,000 to 6,000 over the five-year period.

The managers of an averaged ILGIC, on the other hand, would compute the average of the five year-end closing numbers (6,500, 7,000, 7,500, 8,000, 6,000) — exactly 7,000 — and then assume that 7,000 is the final value of the index. The formula would then divide 7,000 by the base level of 6,000. The result, 1.17, constitutes a 17% gain. Hence, the final payoff in this scenario would be $117 for every $100 invested.

Thus, it appears that averaging, in this case, is better than no averaging, because it provides a form of protection against a disastrous 2002.

But herein lies the key to the discussion: hindsight. With perfect hindsight, or *ex post*, as the economists say, it is easy to determine which product you would rather have bought to begin with. Naturally, in the 2002 crash scenario, the averaging formula would have been preferred. On the other hand, in the first and rosier scenario, the non-averaging formula would have yielded better results. It all depends on the path taken by the stock market during the five years.

But here's the clincher: Overwhelmingly, the odds are that the non-averaging formula will produce a better result. Mathematical proof of this is beyond the scope of this book. The averaging does provide additional protection, but it's not really necessary because you already have downside protection.

Let's summarize the discussion this way. Given the choice between identical five-year index-linked GICs, one with averaging and one without, I would take the non-averaging product hands down. In fact, the averaging feature, whether it's yearly, quarterly, or monthly, reduces the value of your protection by about 50%. Moreover, the more frequent the averaging, the lower the value of your protection — so that an ILGIC averaged monthly is worth less than an ILGIC averaged yearly, and so on.

Recognizing the reduced value of averaging, many vendors of averaged ILGICs have added some minimal interest and something called a participation factor. The idea is to increase the size of the final payoff by a factor greater than one, so as to make up for the lower value resulting from averaging.

For example, some index-linked GICs offered by credit unions multiply the average increase by 1.5 or 2, and use that number to calculate the final payoff. Hence, in our earlier 2002 doomsday scenario, the payoff interest rate would be 17% x 1.5 = 25.5%, or 17% x 2 = 34%, in some cases. The actual participation factor is determined by the financial institution and tends to change depending on market conditions.

Here is a general representation (formula) for all averaged index-linked GICs:

$$\text{Interest Rate on ILGIC} = \text{Participation Factor} \times \frac{\text{(Average Index Level – Base Index Level)}}{\text{Base Index Level}}$$

If the average index level is lower than the base index level, the downside protection kicks in, and you simply get your principal back.

Locking In. Some companies allow you to "lock in" your investment return at some point during the life of the contract. For example, Scotiabank was recently selling a three-year product, its return based on the performance of a G7 index, without dividends (the G7 index is a basket of stocks from the seven largest industrialized countries in the world). Buyers of this ILGIC could lock in their return on the second anniversary.

Imagine you were one of those buyers. If you purchased the G7 index–linked GIC on January 15, 1998, it would mature on January 15, 2001. However, on January 15, 2000 (give or take a week or two), you could contact the bank and ask them to lock in your return. It's just like locking in a mortgage rate. If the stock market went up or down after the lock-in date, it would have no effect on your investment return. Remember, you wouldn't get your money back on the second anniversary, you would simply lock in a return.

You could use this Scotiabank offering as either a non-registered or a Registered Retirement Savings Plan (RRSP) investment, but you couldn't redeem it prior to maturity. The amount invested would not be considered part of your 20% foreign-content limit; it would also be protected by CDIC insurance.

The payoff from the G7 index–linked GIC would be the higher of 0% and the percentage increase of a weighted market index encompassing each of the G7 countries, up to a specified maximum between 25% and 35%. This maximum return was set at inception and is a function of interest rates and stock market conditions at that time.

The market indices implemented for the seven countries, and their relative weighting within the composite "Scotia G7 Index," are displayed in Table 5.3.

Table 5.3

Scotiabank G7 Index–Linked GIC

Country	Index	Weight
United States	SP500	25%
Japan	Nikkei 225	20%
Germany	DAX30	15%
France	CAC40	15%
U.K.	FTSE100	10%
Canada	TSE35	10%
Italy	MIB30	5%

With this Scotiabank product, you could have a difficult decision to make on your second anniversary: whether or not to lock in your rate of return. Clearly, if the underlying index had not increased much, or for that matter had gone down over the first two years, it would make no sense to lock in a poor or negative return. Things could only get better, and they could not get much worse, thanks to your downside protection. Likewise, if the return had been stellar, or exceeded the cap rate, you should lock in the return, because things could not get any better, and they certainly could get worse. It is the in-between type of scenario that is the most difficult to analyze.

The overall effect of this may be illustrated in Figure 5.4. If you lock in the return, you are giving up the potential gain in exchange for protection from the potential loss.

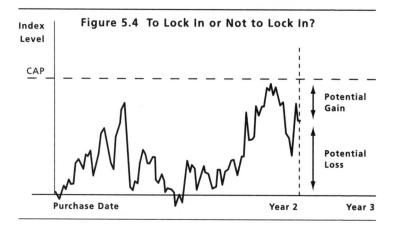

Figure 5.4 To Lock In or Not to Lock In?

In sum, the four main features of ILGICs can add to or subtract from their value, depending on their properties. But generally speaking, an ILGIC will be more valuable if it has a shorter term, a narrow index, a non-averaging formula, and lock-in options. A higher growth cap and participation factor will also make the product more attractive.

Do They Belong in Your Portfolio?

Here, of course, we come to the central question. To answer it, you will have to consider a variety of issues. Here are some of the major factors to review.

Taxes. If held outside an RRSP, index-linked GICs are taxed at the highest ordinary interest-income tax rate, as opposed to the more favourable capital gains rate, which is what would apply to a straight investment in the underlying index. This is a substantial difference — 25% — and should be included in all your break-even calculations. Furthermore, if you hold a three-year ILGIC outside an RRSP, you may incur a tax liability on the accrued interest, even before the contract matures. In plain English, you may have to pay taxes, at the highest marginal tax rate, on money that you haven't yet earned. Consequently, I only see an ILGIC strategy making sense if and when it is held inside your RRSP, where all taxes are deferred until the plan matures.

Time Horizon. When will you need the funds? What is your time horizon? If your time horizon is greater than 10 years, such as inside an RRSP, downside protection over a two- or three-year period seems unnecessary. If, on the other hand, you are saving for a downpayment on a house or for a new car, the index-linked GIC gives you valuable shortfall protection, and makes some sense given that shorter horizon.

Liquidity. What if an emergency arises and you need the funds tomorrow? A mutual fund or a stock portfolio can always be liquidated. Regrettably, that's not the case with index-linked GICs.

Size of Portfolio. The larger your investment portfolio, the cheaper it is to purchase downside protection from other sources. The next chapter will explain how you can design your own downside insurance policy.

Risk Aversion. How averse are you to downside risk?

Why is preservation of principal so important? Remember, your principal is a nominal quantity that will be eroded due to inflation by the time the ILGIC matures. If you invest $1,000 and the worst that can happen is that you get $1,000 back in five years, some people erroneously conclude that they can't lose. However, you must remember that $1,000 in five years' time is worth a lot less than $1,000 today. (Which would you rather have?) Personally, if I invested $1,000 today and got back $1,000 in five years, I would feel that I lost the interest I could have earned in a risk-free bank deposit.

CONCLUSION

If you are (1) relatively new to the equity markets and would like to get your feet wet with small sums of money; (2) have a short time horizon for the investment; and (3) are very risk-averse on the downside, index-linked GICs are a marvellous way to get involved, especially inside an RRSP or RRIF, where tax isn't an issue. Indeed, index-linked GICs have been fondly labelled "index funds with training wheels." And that's not a bad analogy.

On the other hand, for relatively sophisticated individuals with a long investment time horizon and sums greater than $10,000 to invest, and for those who really want the benefits of an index-linked GIC, it may make greater sense to ask your financial planner or broker to help you "cook it at home" for less. Chapter 6 shows you how.

Can You Cook Downside
Protection at Home?

In the last few chapters, I have been describing a range of investment products that in one way or another let you invest in the equity markets — but with downside protection. By downside protection, I mean that your original principal will be guaranteed, regardless of how the underlying stock markets perform over the period. If the market increases, your money grows; if the market falls, you get your money back.

For example, with a segregated mutual fund, your downside protection kicks in after 10 years or at death. Likewise, with index-linked GICs, your downside protection will take effect when the ILGIC matures, in two to five years.

The downside protection does not come free. You have to pay for it, in most cases with higher management fees, or sometimes implicitly with an unfavourable tax treatment, forfeited interest, dividends, and potential growth.

Reading the previous chapters, you might have come to the conclusion that the only way to build downside protection — to have your investment cake and eat it too — is by turning your money over to a bank, trust company, insurance company, or mutual fund.

In fact — and this is the subject I will explore in this chapter — you can probably invest directly in the stock market and "cook" your own downside protection at home, without buying any of the above-mentioned products sold by financial institutions.

A good example is the index-linked GIC. You can effectively create your own (say) $10,000 investment in an ILGIC by buying, for the same total price, (1) financial products that provide the potential for stock market growth, and (2) financial products that replicate the downside protection ILGICs provide. Does the home-cooked method confer any benefits? Indeed, it does. You gain by cooking at home because ILGICs are illiquid and any gains made on them (outside an RRSP) are subject to ordinary interest-income tax rates; the alternative "cooked" products, however, have high liquidity and yield gains that are subject to the more favourable capital gains tax. Furthermore, if the sum of money is large enough, you may even gain by getting products (1) and (2) for less than what you would have to invest in an index-linked GIC.

Moreover, at the same time, you are guaranteeing that your principal will remain intact, even though you are exposing yourself to the ravages of national and international equity markets. Of course, if you choose this route, you will still incur costs; that is unavoidable. But in many cases, the costs will be lower than those implicit in index-linked GICs and on Seg funds.

I should note at the outset that although these strategies

will reduce your odds of regret, their implementation can be somewhat complicated; they are, therefore, not for everybody. In fact, you might want to skip this chapter on a first reading, and come back to it at a later time. And please bear in mind that if you *do* decide to cook at home, you *will* need a standard brokerage account and possibly the help of an investment adviser licensed to sell options.

I must also be careful to distinguish between the downside protection derived from index-linked GICs and the downside protection conferred by segregated mutual funds. The Seg funds — in addition to the maturity guarantee — provide you with a downside-protected death benefit that is virtually impossible to create without an insurance company (although you can always create a specific death benefit by purchasing a term life insurance policy). In any case, the protection of an index-linked GIC is easier to create yourself. In fact, despite the technicalities, almost any index-linked GIC now on the market today can be cooked — or at the very least closely mimicked — at home. The formula is standard, and the ingredients are few.

With that preamble, I'd now like to show you *two* alternative ways in which a two-year $10,000 Toronto Stock Exchange 35 index–linked GIC with a 20% growth cap can be replicated. I picked this one because it is one of the more popular ILGICs in Canada today. You will have to trust me that alternative indices, maturities, and payout structures can be handled in a similar fashion.

Let's deal first with the downside protection. We know that the regular ILGIC contains built-in downside protection — in two years, you are guaranteed to receive $10,000. But the same downside protection can be created by purchasing something called a zero-coupon bond.

A zero-coupon (federal or provincial) bond is a bond with no coupons or interest payments attached. Unlike a regular federal or provincial bond that entitles you to semi-annual coupons, a zero-coupon bond will provide you with absolutely no interest payments over its life. At maturity, all you will get is the face value of the bond, which can be $1,000, $10,000, or even $100,000.

Wait a minute, you say. No coupons? No interest payments? Why would I ever buy such a bond from the government? Don't I pay enough in taxes?

Well, here's the point, subtle though it may be. Although zero-coupon bonds give you no interest payments along the way, you *will* get implicit interest payments at maturity. That's because zero-coupon bonds *always sell* for less than face value. In other words, you will always pay less than $1,000, $10,000, or $100,000 for the bond that matures at $1,000, $10,000, or $100,000. Hence, because you are paying less than its maturity value, you are earning (as *de facto* interest compensation) the difference between the purchase price and the maturity value.

For example, right now you could pay $9,000 to buy a Government of Canada zero-coupon bond that is guaranteed to mature at $10,000 in two years. The guaranteed gain from this transaction is $1,000 and represents an interest rate of $1,000/$9,000 = 11.1% for two years, or a compounded 5.4% per year.

Essentially, a zero-coupon bond functions like a compounded GIC, where the interest is implicitly re-invested. Although you can't get more than a five-year GIC from a bank or trust company in Canada, you can buy zero-coupon bonds with maturities that stretch out as far as 25 — or sometimes even 30 — years. Again, there will be no interest payments for 25 years, but the waiting will pay off at maturity.

For example, today you can buy a 25-year Government of Canada zero-coupon bond for $2,600, which is guaranteed to mature at $10,000 in 25 years. Sounds impressive, doesn't it? You pay just $2,600 and get $10,000 back. Is there some sort of catch? Is this a pyramid scheme? Not at all. Remember, you won't get any money back for 25 years, so the compensation must be large. Here, in this instance, the guaranteed gain is $7,400 and represents a compound interest rate of approximately 5.5% for the next 25 years.

Now, even though the bonds don't mature for 25 years, that doesn't mean you can't *sell* them for 25 years. In fact, you can probably sell them at any time of day or night by calling your broker — who probably bought them for you in the first place — and placing an order to sell. Of course, you won't get $10,000 — for that you must wait until maturity. But more likely than not, you'll get more than you paid.

Unfortunately, the tax treatment of these zero-coupon bonds can get messy, if they are held outside an RRSP. When you buy a zero-coupon bond, Revenue Canada considers you as having implicitly received interest each and every year you hold the bond, even though you don't get your money back until maturity (or when you sell it).

The reason I'm going on about these zero-coupon bonds is that they are a perfect way to guarantee a lump sum of money at some point in the future. For example, if you want to make sure that you have exactly $10,000 in exactly 10 years, you can buy a zero-coupon bond, today, for about $5,800, hold the bond for a decade, until maturity, and you will then get the $10,000 from (and backed by) the federal government.

Notice, however, that you only need about $5,800 today to get the $10,000 at maturity. You obviously don't need the full $10,000. The important thing to remember is that if you have $10,000 that you want to invest in the stock market for 10 years, but you want downside protection on the $10,000, you can get it with zero-coupon bonds. So, you can set aside $5,800 — i.e., by buying zero-coupon bonds that mature at $10,000 — and use the remaining $4,200 to invest in the stock market. Even if you lose the *entire* $4,200 (not terribly likely), you are still guaranteed to receive the $10,000 bond payment in 10 years.

Now, let's return to our two-year ILGIC example. To cook one yourself, you're going to buy a Government of Canada zero-coupon bond for $9,000, guaranteed to mature at $10,000 in two years. The *guaranteed* gain from this transaction is $1,000 and represents an interest rate of $1,000/$9,000 = 11.1% for two years, or a compound 5.4% for one year.

But what about the upside potential of ILGICs? How can that be replicated at home? The answer involves the use of financial instruments known as options.

Options are traded, listed, bought, and sold on an options exchange, which is usually located right next door to a stock exchange. Toronto and Montreal have large option markets. There are two basic types of options — calls and puts.

A call option is a contract that gives you the right, but not the obligation, to *buy* shares of an underlying stock at a pre-specified fixed price. For example, if you buy a contract of 100 Newbridge call options, you then have the right, but not the obligation, to buy 100 shares of Newbridge stock at a pre-determined price during a pre-specified period of time.

To be more specific, you can pay $400 now to purchase the right, but not the obligation, to pay another $3,000 to acquire 100 shares of Newbridge sometime over the next six months. In this example, the $400 is called the options premium and the $3,000 is usually referred to as the option's strike price. If the price of 100 shares goes above $3,000 in the next six months, you would want to exercise your call option; at that point, you can hold on to the shares, or you can turn around and sell the shares right away for a quick return. On the other hand, if the price of 100 shares stays the same or goes down in the next six months, you will "strike out" or lose on the original investment. Obviously, you will only exercise the call option when the price of 100 shares of Newbridge is above the strike price of $3,000. After all, why would you pay more than it was worth? If the value is above the strike price, it is called "being in the money."

So there are two prices (or numbers) to monitor: the price at which you purchase the 100 Newbridge call options (the $400 premium), and the price at which the options allow you to purchase 100 shares of Newbridge (the $3,000 strike price). These two numbers, however, represent very different things.

In fact, there is nothing special about the $3,000 strike price; it could have been higher — $3,500, for example — or lower ($2,500). If you think about it for a minute, you will agree that the lower the strike price at which the call option contract allows you to buy Newbridge, the more you must pay for this right. In other words, the lower the strike price, the higher the premium. Indeed, it's not uncommon to see three or four different call options trading on a stock like Newbridge, each with its own strike price. For example, you might see the $2,500 strike price selling for $700, and the $3,500 strike price selling for $200.

Here's another term to understand: An "out-of-the-money" call is a call option with a strike price that is above the current price of the underlying stock at the time the call is purchased. For example, if Newbridge is trading at $30 per share, a call option with a strike price of $36 per share would be 20% out-of-the-money (the $6 differential being one-fifth, or 20%, of the current trading price). A call option with a strike price of $33 per share would be 10% out-of-the-money. A call option with a strike price of exactly $30 per share is said to be at-the-money.

Now let's take a look at put options.

A put option is the exact opposite of a call option. A put

is a contract that gives you the right, but not the obligation, to *sell* shares of the underlying stock at a fixed price over a pre-specified period. Thus, if you buy a put on Newbridge, you have the right, but not the obligation, to sell 100 shares of Newbridge stock during a particular window of time and at a certain price.

For example, you can pay $350 now to purchase the right, but not the obligation, to sell 100 shares of Newbridge at $3,000, sometime over the next six months. Once again, the $350 is called the put option premium; the $3,000 is referred to as the put option strike price. In the puts case, if the price of 100 shares of Newbridge does not fall below $3,000 in the next six months, you will "strike out," or lose on the original investment. Put options are the stock market equivalent of car insurance. When you insure your $20,000 car, you have essentially acquired the right (but definitely not the obligation) to demolish your car and then sell it back to the insurance company for $20,000. Some people choose a $1,000 deductible, so the strike price is only $19,000, which leads to lower premiums.

You do not need to own shares of a particular stock in order to buy an option. In fact, just like a regular stock, the options exchange lets you buy and sell puts and calls anytime over the life of the option. Thus, you can make (or lose) money without ever having to buy or sell the underlying stock.

In addition to options on individual stocks, you can also buy and sell puts and calls on gold, silver, foreign currencies, stock indices, and even commodities like pork bellies and heating oil. Bought and sold on an options exchange, these options give you the right, but not the obligation, to buy (with a call) and/or sell (with a put) a fixed quantity of the underlying security at a fixed price.

Why the long lecture on options?

Well, it's safe to assume that banks, trust companies,

and credit unions "hedge" every index-linked GIC they sell to the public using the financial instruments I've just been describing; in other words, these institutions are financially engineering the product. For an ILGIC with a 20% growth cap, for example, they probably take a portion of your deposit, buy a zero-coupon bond (for downside protection), sell 20% out-of-the-money calls, and buy at-the-money calls. And my argument simply is that if the banks, trust companies, and credit unions can do it, so can you.

We've already seen how you can create your own downside protection, or guarantee, by paying $9,000 to buy some two-year zero-coupon bonds that will mature at $10,000. Now you can use the remaining $1,000 to get the call options you need to replicate the upside potential of an ILGIC.

Specifically, you will need to purchase two-year at-the-money call options on about $10,000 worth of TSE35 index stock and sell an equal number of two-year 20% out-of-the-money call options on the same stock. This, and only this, combination will create the upward participation you need — but with the 20% cap — just like the index-linked GIC. You could choose a different underlying index or stock, as long as it is highly correlated with the index linked to the ILGIC you're interested in mimicking.

You buy the two-year at-the-money call options because at maturity, if the price of the TSE35 index has gone up, you can exercise those call options to realize a profit equal to the difference between the new maturity price and your at-the-money strike price. This represents your upward participation.

You *sell* two-year 20% out-of-the-money call options to generate income *now* from the premium. But what will happen at maturity, if the TSE35 stock price goes above 20%, is this: The buyer of your call options will gleefully exercise the call, so you will owe him or her the difference between (a) the high, maturity-date stock price and (b) 120% of the underlying stock price at the date you sold the options.

So your at-the-money calls fully exposed you to the gains in the stock price, but your obligations from the sale of your out-of-the-money call options mean you have to pay someone else the proceeds beyond 20%. This represents your 20% growth cap.

A broker can give you the precise numbers — but roughly speaking at the time of writing, the at-the-money call would *cost you* $1,500, and selling the out-of-the-money calls would *net you* $500. Do the math and you are left with a bill of $1,000 for the options — which you pay with the $1,000 left over from the purchase of the zero-coupon bond.

In reality the option prices would fluctuate hourly — and you may get slightly different results from the above — but hopefully the idea is clear.

Also, in our example, we did not include any brokerage fees or transaction costs, so the numbers were biased somewhat. In other words, you may earn less than $500 from selling the 20% out-of-the-money call option and you may have to pay more than $1,500 for the at-the-money call option — when you take into account the brokerage fees. But my goal here is to give you a general sense of how this strategy would work — not to give you precise numbers for your profit and loss.

In fact, I'm pretty certain that for sums of money less than $10,000, the commissions, transaction costs, and fees attached to trying to replicate the product at home can be prohibitive. Indeed, the providers of index-linked GICs (buying wholesale versus buying retail) use their economies of scale to purchase these "options" at a better overall price than you, as a small investor, could ever hope to obtain.

On the other hand, for sums greater than $10,000, you

can probably cook it — or a very similar product — at home for less.

Now, as you may recall, I mentioned earlier that there are *two* distinct ways to create your own ILGIC-like downside protection and growth potential. Here is another strategy that may be even better than the zero-coupon-plus-call-option combo.

Indeed, perhaps a simpler alternative to buying a generic TSE35 index–linked GIC is to purchase TIPS, traded on the Toronto Stock Exchange, together with some put options for protection.

What are TIPS?

TIPS is an acronym for Toronto Index Participation UnitS. They are very similar in structure and purpose to an equity mutual fund, with a few key differences. First, this mutual fund always has 35 stocks in it. No more, no less. These 35 stocks are the largest capitalization stocks traded on the Toronto Stock Exchange. Given the automatic nature of its holding, with TIPS, there is no fund manager checking the market daily, deciding what and when to buy and sell.

Second, like closed-end mutual funds, TIPS are actually traded on a stock exchange, so you can buy and sell these units at any time during the trading day. Finally, just like Newbridge, or any other stock, you can buy and sell put and call options on TIPS.

Here's a simplified example of how you can use TIPS to create an ILGIC-type product. You have $10,000 to invest for two years. You want to expose yourself to some upside market potential, but want to avoid the downside risk. You check the newspaper's business section and find that each TIPS unit sells for $35.

So you buy 285 TIPS for a total cost of $10,000. That takes care of the potential upside. If the price of each TIP rises to $40 in two years, you'll have made $1,425 (285 x $5). And in the meantime, you are entitled to receive full dividends with a favourable tax treatment, to pay capital gains taxes only upon disposition of the shares, and to enjoy complete liquidity — i.e., the ability to sell at any time.

But what about the downside? To protect your investment, you *could* decide to buy put options on your TIPS. Remember, the equity put option is like an insurance contract that protects your principal for the life of the option. In this case, you could buy 285 units of two-year puts, each with a strike price of $35, and a market premium of $3.16 — which is quoted from a broker — for a total cost of approximately $900 (285 x $3.16). That means that if the unit price of TIPS falls to $30 or even to $25 during that year, you still have the option to sell your TIPS for your original $35 per unit. (Once again, please remember that these prices tend to fluctuate hourly.) Of course, if the price of TIPS goes up, you won't exercise your puts, but your TIPS are doing well, so you're happy.

Now, here is the problem. To buy those "protective puts" you would have to spend an additional $900. That's fair — but what if you don't want to commit an additional $900 to protect your $10,000? In fact, doesn't the index-linked GIC protect your $10,000 without requiring any more money?

Well, there is a way to protect your $10,000 invested in the stock market — without dishing out an additional $900 for the puts. The way to do this is by giving up some of your rights. Specifically, you would have to give up your right to any appreciation above 20% and essentially give up your right to any dividends.

More specifically, you could finance part of the puts purchase (and lose your yield above 20%) by selling 285 units of 20% out-of-the-money call options. This is the same strategy used in the zero-coupon-plus-calls scenario to finance the protective at-the-money calls. An out-of-the-money call, you'll remember, is a call option with a strike price that is above the current price of the underlying stock. If our strike price in this example is $35, the strike price of the call option will be $42 (120% of $35). You get a premium for selling these calls, but if the price of TIPS goes above $42 at the end of your two years, the buyer is going to exercise their options, and you'll have to pay them the difference (anything over 20%). This "skimming" effect is your 20% growth cap.

In current market conditions — according to broker quotes — by selling these 285 units of 20% out-of-the-money calls, you will receive about $500 (285 x the premium price of $1.75). So you now have to finance only $400 ($900 – $500) to buy the protective puts. But with a bit of luck, you can expect to receive $400 worth of dividends from the 285 TIPS that you are holding outright.

So what do you have when the day is over? You have 285 units of TIPS, plus 285 put options, struck at $35 to protect those TIPS. And you have sold 285 call options with a strike price of $42 to finance part of the put purchase. The dividends from the TIPS should, it is hoped, finance the rest — which is why I said you are giving up the dividends. You are giving them up as they arrive — to pay for the original puts.

Is this TIPS-plus-puts combination simpler than the zero-coupon strategy?

I would say that this strategy is a bit easier to understand, and has a more preferential tax treatment because you essentially own equity investments that entitle you to capital gains and the dividend tax credit.

So here you have it. I have demonstrated *two ways* to replicate the payoff from a two-year, TSE35 index–linked GIC with a 20% cap.

Bear in mind, though, that for more complex index-linked GICs, with averaging or lock-in features, the ingredients and instructions for the do-it-yourself strategy can be quite complicated, and perhaps should be avoided for that reason alone. But I assure you that if the value of your portfolio is large enough, a knowledgeable broker or financial adviser should be able to structure a product that yields a payoff virtually identical to the payoff from any ILGIC on the market today — probably at a cheaper price or better terms — and with much greater liquidity. In fact, if the GIC is linked to the U.S.-based SP500 index, or a Europe-based index, you can actually buy the equivalent of international TIPS on the American and New York stock exchanges. (They have cute names like SPiDRS and WEBS.)

Remember the main benefit here. You can't cash the ILGIC before it matures, but you can always sell the bonds, the options, and the index basket, whenever you want.

From a tax perspective, any profits from trading in index options will be taxed at the more favourable capital gains rate. (There is one exception: If you have "an adventure or concern in the nature of trade," which, according to Revenue Canada, means that you are not simply an investor, but a professional who makes his or her living buying and selling options, you will pay ordinary income rates.) Similarly, if the market falls and the options expire worthless, the option premium paid is tax-deductible.

So if you take the TIPS-plus-puts route, you will be much better off compared with ILGICs when they are outside an RRSP. The zero-coupon-bond-plus-call option, on the other hand, will create a slightly more onerous tax predicament. But it is still better than the tax treatment on an index-linked GIC. The issuers of index-linked GICs should have pressed Revenue Canada to bifurcate or partition profits from an ILGIC into their ordinary interest and capital gains components, as is done in the United States by the Internal Revenue Service.

In sum, I agree — and you probably noticed — that the self-constructed strategy is not for everybody. Many consumers are delighted with the performance of their index-linked GICs thus far, and I wish them continued happiness. In general, my philosophy is that financial products cannot be classified as either good or bad. Rather, they can be good or bad for particular situations, depending on your personal circumstances and where you are in your life cycle. Table 6.1 displays the features of these different ways of structuring a financial product that has limited upside potential with no downside risk.

Table 6.1

The Alternatives

	Liquidity	Tax	Dividend	Complex	Total Cost
Zero Bond + Call Option	High	O.I. + C.G.	None	Yes	Med
TIPS + Put Option	High	C.G.	Yes	Yes	High
ILGIC	Low	O.I.	None	No	Low

CONCLUSION

The possibility of financial regret drives many consumers to acquire investment products that provide upside participation together with downside protection. The purpose of this chapter was to show that downside investment protection can be obtained independently using equity and index options known as puts and calls.

The benefit of this type of downside protection is that it provides greater liquidity and flexibility than an index-linked GIC or even a segregated mutual fund. In fact, if your investment is large enough, you can probably get it cheaper as well.

Of course, the real cost of the do-it-yourself approach is the time, effort, and complexity that these strategies entail. And only you can decide whether the potential savings and benefits justify those costs.

Borrowing to Invest:
Pay Down Mortgage or Top Up RRSP?

It's bonus time — and your boss has finally rewarded you for your hard work and loyalty. What a bonanza! — $10,000. And there are so many tempting toys to acquire. But suddenly you are seized by a rare fit of fiscal prudence. And instead of that Caribbean vacation, you decide to put the funds to better use — financial planning. But what exactly should you do with the money? Should you pay down your home mortgage debt? Or should you finally make use of that extra Registered Retirement Savings Plan (RRSP) room that you have never managed to fill? Decisions, decisions.

One of the questions most commonly asked by investors who hold both extra cash and a home mortgage is whether that money should be allocated toward paying down the mortgage or whether it should be invested in an RRSP — provided you have the extra room.

This is not a trivial question. That's partly because there are obvious benefits to both strategies. Reducing your mortgage can save you tens of thousands of dollars in interest payments; investing in your RRSP can save you thousands in taxes — and help accumulate funds for your retirement. Moreover, because RRSPs and home mortgages are totally different types of financial instruments, it's difficult to immediately perceive a basis upon which to compare them.

A fair bit of ink has been spilled in the popular press in recent years to focus on precisely this issue — the choice between the two. Regrettably, some of the advice has been quite appalling. My goal — in the first part of the chapter — is to examine both sides of the mortgage/RRSP coin. Hopefully, I can add some value to the debate by examining the odds that you will regret either choice.

In the second part of the chapter, I want to examine a related question — leverage. Under what circumstances does it make sense to borrow money to invest? How risky is that strategy? What are the odds that using leverage will pay off for you?

But first: the mortgage-versus-RRSP question.

By now, you may already be able to anticipate my bias: I simply don't believe that there is a single right or wrong answer. As I've said in an earlier chapter, most of the factors that determine your financial future are random or simply unknown. The success or failure of any financial decision, therefore, will generally depend on what the future holds. As such, we can only examine the odds that we will (or won't) regret a specific decision. The mortgage/RRSP dilemma, then, is about which one will give you the better odds — as opposed to which option is the superior choice.

For those of you who are slightly impatient, I'm going to jump ahead and make the following statement about the mortgage-versus-RRSP decision. *If you expect the long-term return from your RRSP investments to be greater than the interest rate you pay on your mortgage, the odds are you will be better off contributing to your RRSP — despite the fact that the interest on the mortgage is not tax-deductible.*

However, before considering the detailed benefits of each strategy, let's make sure we're clear about the characteristics of each of these financial choices.

A mortgage, of course, is essentially a loan. Like other loans, a mortgage represents a personal pledge by the borrower that it will be repaid. However, unlike other loans, the lender's confidence that he or she will be repaid is not based on the investor's overall or personal financial health; it's based on the property that effectively underwrites the mortgage. If you (the home owner) fail to meet your mortgage payments, the lender has the right to "foreclose" on the property — that is, the lender can take title to your house, sell it off, and pocket the amount owed by you, the borrower.

Just for the record, the basic components of a mortgage are as follows:

1. *The principal*: the total amount borrowed or outstanding;
2. *The mortgage rate*: the interest rate on the principal;
3. *The mortgage payment*: the regular installment of cash with which you repay the mortgage;
4. *The amortization period*: the number of years it will take to completely repay the mortgage;
5. *The term*: the period of time covered by a specific mortgage agreement. When the term matures, the mortgage is renegotiated at prevailing interest rates. Hence,

while the amortization period may be 25 years, terms
are much shorter, usually ranging from six months to
five years;
6. *Home equity*: the value of the home above (or below)
the outstanding principal of the mortgage.

The mortgage payment, incidentally, is not simply
the interest on the loan. In most situations, it includes both
interest and principal components. In other words, your
cash payments on a mortgage are structured so that, instead
of simply paying interest at regular intervals and repaying
the original principal at the end of the mortgage, each
interval payment includes both an interest payment and
some principal repayment.

The operating principle of a mortgage is quite simple. You
initially receive a lump sum of cash, and then are obliged
to repay it over time, in a combined series of principal and
interest repayments. If you fail to make these payments,
foreclosure will take place. Then, the property will be
sold, and your equity used to make a lump-sum payment,
reducing if not eliminating the remaining balance owed.

In many mortgage agreements, of course, you have the
right to pay down a portion of your principal. When and if
you did so, you could then renegotiate (downward) the
amount paid each month. Alternatively, you could keep
the same total monthly payment, but finish paying off your
mortgage much earlier than originally expected. In other
words, with the reduction in the principal, you can change
(in your favour) the ratio of principal and interest calculated
into each payment. As more and more of your principal
declined, more and more of each monthly or weekly payment would go toward paying off the balance; less and less
would go toward interest payments.

Remember, by paying down your mortgage, you are
reducing your debt load. If you don't pay down your mort-

gage, your debt load will remain the same. In the same way, you could just as easily *add* to your debt load by *increasing the principal* — or size — of your mortgage. (This is sometimes referred to as a second mortgage.)

Here's where it's helpful to look at the mortgage/RRSP question from a slightly different perspective. It's my contention that if you decide *not* to pay down your mortgage — and instead contribute to your RRSP — you are essentially or effectively deciding to borrow money to make the RRSP contribution. Why? Well, if you pay down your mortgage, you will reduce your debt load; that we know. If you don't reduce your mortgage, you are using money that you could have used to reduce your debt load, to contribute to an RRSP. This means that you are implicitly borrowing money.

Think about it this way. Assume that you owe $100,000 on your home mortgage and you get a $10,000 bonus. Now, if you contribute the $10,000 to your RRSP, you will still owe $100,000. If, on the other hand, you pay down your mortgage, you will owe only $90,000. If you then go to your bank, take out an RRSP loan for $10,000, and contribute that $10,000 to an RRSP, you are back exactly where you started. You owe $90,000 + $10,000 = $100,000 and you have a $10,000 RRSP. The interest payments that you make on the house are not (generally) tax-deductible. Nor will the interest payments on the RRSP loan be tax-deductible.

Thus, from a purely monetary perspective, I view the decision of whether to pay down your mortgage or invest in your RRSP as perfectly synonymous with whether to borrow money to invest in an RRSP; hence the title of this chapter, "Borrowing to Invest."

So — to jump ahead again — if we agree that it's prudent to borrow in order to contribute to an RRSP, then it is equally prudent to not pay down your mortgage and contribute to an RRSP instead. An RRSP, as you probably know, is a legal method of deferring taxes. Every year, an investor is allowed to contribute 18% of earned income, up to a maximum of $13,500, to his or her RRSP. The legal structure of the plan must be set up at a financial institution. The amount contributed is deducted from that year's income. An RRSP, then, is a tax-deferral system; it's not a perpetual tax shelter. The RRSP must be converted by age 69. The tax treatment of the withdrawn RRSP funds depends on the subsequent investment plan. See Chapter 9 for more details.

From the above discussion, it is clear that mortgages and RRSPs are different structures. Both involve a series of payments, but the reasons for these payments are completely different. It is not surprising, therefore, that the incentives for using extra cash either to reduce a mortgage or invest in an RRSP are completely different as well.

As I said, regular mortgage payments consist of both interest and principal, blended together. The benefit of using extra cash to make extra mortgage payments is twofold. First, the total principal owing will be reduced. This is obvious. If you put $10,000 toward a mortgage of $100,000, you will now owe $90,000.

Second, because you now owe $90,000 and not $100,000, you may rightfully ask the bank to reduce your monthly payments. Alternatively, you could keep the same total monthly payments, but (based on the new $90,000 principal amount) more of it will be allocated to principal and less to interest. In other words, the interest owing will now be calculated on the new, lower principal outstanding. In this case, instead of paying off your mortgage completely in, say, 10 years, you'd be paying it off in eight years, giving you two years' worth of cash to use for non-mortgage purposes.

The decision on what to do with your payments is up to you. However, in the discussion that follows, I'll assume — just for the sake of argument — that *if* you decide to pay down your mortgage, you will reduce your subsequent monthly payments.

On the flip side, by using the extra cash to invest in your RRSP — assuming that the RRSP maximum has not yet been reached — you are tying up cash, and happily so, for three good reasons. First, you receive the tax savings discussed earlier. Second, the funds are allowed to grow inside the plan tax-free, until they are withdrawn. Third, by putting aside this extra cash, you will be better prepared financially for retirement.

So, when making this difficult decision — using extra cash to pay down a mortgage or to invest in an RRSP — you must recognize the trade-off that takes place. By investing in an RRSP, you reduce taxes and increase retirement savings, both very important long-term goals. By doing so, however, you are unable to decrease regular mortgage payments.

Of course, you could always take the monthly savings created by paying down a mortgage and invest that amount in an RRSP. In other words, if using a $10,000 bonus to pay down the mortgage resulted in an immediate monthly $100 mortgage reduction for the next 10 years, the monthly $100 could be invested in an RRSP until retirement.

And indeed, this is the fundamental, more specific question: *Is it better to use a windfall of cash to pay down the mortgage and use the consequent reduction in mortgage payments to increase RRSP investment? Or is it better to use the extra cash to invest in an RRSP immediately?*

It is only after we phrase the question in this way — on equal footing — that the comparison makes sense. In fact, another way to phrase the question could have been as follows: Should you contribute to your RRSP now — in one lump sum — or should you contribute to your RRSP later — in monthly installments?

To answer this question, I offer below an example of a mathematical model; the method I use will enable you to calculate whether you're better off paying down your mortgage or investing in an RRSP. But be warned: this fundamental question has been the subject of much discussion over the years. At one time, you would have been strongly advised to pay down the mortgage as quickly as possible. In recent years, you would have been urged to invest in an RRSP.

Why all the talk, you might ask, if a model can provide the solution? The answer is that there are several factors that the model does not take into account. These include feelings of security, liquidity, risk tolerance, and diversification. The model cannot take these factors into account, because they depend on the individual investor. After presenting the model, I will consider these issues in more detail.

Let's consider a particular example — Frank Wilson. Some 15 years ago, Frank entered into a mortgage with a 25-year amortization period; hence, the time remaining on this mortgage is 10 years. The interest rate associated with the mortgage is 9% (compounded monthly), and the payments are $1,257.30 per month. This works out to a principal outstanding of exactly $100,000. Frank has 20 years until retirement and pays a marginal tax rate of 50%. Frank expects to receive — and this is a crucial assumption — an annual 10% return on his investments. Frank generally does not contribute his RRSP maximum, and Frank can repay mortgage principal without penalty. Note that the expected return on investment is higher, by one percentage point, than the interest rate on the mortgage.

One fine day, Frank receives a $10,000 inheritance from a forgotten great aunt. Should Frank invest the $10,000 in an RRSP immediately? Or should he pay down his mortgage and then contribute the monthly savings to an RRSP? To answer this question, I will determine how much cash Frank will have in 20 years following either strategy. After discussing this specific situation, I will explain the model used to obtain the results. If one strategy will yield more cash than the other, then Frank should (it would seem obvious) choose the strategy with the better payoff.

To begin, let's consider how much the $10,000 will grow into should Frank choose to invest it immediately in an RRSP. Frank can actually contribute $20,000 — not $10,000 — to his RRSP. Why? By contributing $20,000, Frank's income for tax purposes is reduced by $20,000; because he's in a 50% tax bracket, he will save $10,000 in taxes.

Thus, if he contributes $20,000, he saves $10,000, making the *effective cost* of the RRSP contribution $10,000 — exactly equal to the $10,000 he inherited. In 20 years, at retirement, Frank's investment of $20,000 will grow into $146,561 — at the expected annual rate of return (compounded monthly) of 10%. So, by deciding to invest in an RRSP immediately, Frank has $146,562 at retirement. Remember, though, there are taxes to pay at that time. If Frank is still in the 50% marginal tax bracket — and he withdraws the money from the RRSP — he will be left with half, or $73,281.

Next, let's consider how much the $10,000 would grow into if used to pay down the mortgage and the monthly savings are invested in the RRSP. By paying down the mortgage by $10,000, Frank could reduce his monthly mortgage payments from $1,257.30 to $1,131.60 — for monthly savings of $125.70. Using the same reasoning as before, twice this amount ($251.40) is invested monthly, 12 times a year, for a 10-year period — the remaining life of the mortgage. This amount will grow into an RRSP of $140,606 at maturity — in 20 years. After taxes, this becomes $70,303.

Clearly, Frank would be better off investing in an RRSP immediately, because he would have $73,281 – $70,303 = $2,978 more at retirement (after tax).

Table 7.1 shows you the results of Frank's decision, for different mortgage rates and investment rates.

For example, in the above scenario, if Frank's mortgage

Table 7.1*

Gain in 20 Years: By How Much Is RRSP Top-Up Better?

(If Investor Contributes $10,000 to an RRSP Now Instead of Paying Down Mortgage and Contributing the Savings Later)

	Investment Rate				
	6%	7%	8%	9%	10%
Mortgage Rate					
6%	$0	$1,738	$4,111	$7,295	$11,513
7%	–$1,488	$0	$2,080	$4,921	$8,736
8%	–$3,013	–$1,780	$0	$2,489	$5,890
9%	–$4,574	–$3,603	–$2,129	$0	$2,978

Note: The numbers in this table assume $100,000 mortgage principal with 10 years remaining in the amortization period. Positive numbers mean that you have more from contributing to an RRSP; negative numbers mean that you have less.

rate is 7% — instead of 9% — and his RRSP earns 10%, then he will have $8,736 more from investing in the RRSP than if he were to pay down the mortgage. If, on the other hand, the mortgage rate is 7% and the rate of return from the RRSP is 6%, then Frank will have $1,488 *less* — in 20 years — if he decides to contribute to the RRSP instead of paying down the mortgage. The negative sign means that you will end up with a deficit of that amount — if you contribute to the RRSP. The zero numbers in the table imply that you are just as well off contributing to the RRSP as you are paying down the mortgage. Intuitively this should make sense, since the interest rates are the same.

Now, you can clearly see the following trend: the lower the mortgage rate, the more desirable the immediate RRSP investment. Similarly, the higher the expectation of returns from the RRSP investment, the more desirable the immediate RRSP investment. This result is not surprising. One can, as I suggested earlier, interpret an immediate RRSP investment (instead of paying down the mortgage) as "borrowing" money at the mortgage rate and using it to invest in an RRSP. True, no cash is actually being borrowed. But by not paying down the mortgage, you are effectively borrowing. Of course, borrowing from one source to invest in another will become more attractive as the rate of interest for borrowing falls and the rate of return for investment rises.

Now we've seen that the question of whether to pay down a mortgage or invest in an RRSP can be answered using a mathematical model, not just by relying on the unsupported advice of financial commentators. You should keep in mind, though, that the various assumptions of the model (e.g., size of principal, amortization period, etc.) do not apply to every situation, so your calculations, and your answers, may not always be so cut-and-dried. And there are some other, more fundamental issues that may cloud the picture somewhat. These relate to the individual investor facing the decision. While investing now in an RRSP may be a better financial decision, the extra money available to the investor at retirement may not be as valuable as the sense of security derived by paying down a mortgage early. So if both investment and mortgage rates are equal, paying down a mortgage may have no benefit from a strictly financial point of view. But from a sense of security viewpoint, there may be great benefits.

I assume, moreover, that investors make decisions based on expectations. But expectations are associated with risk. For example, I have assumed an expected return of 10% per year on RRSP investments. But does that payoff, considered along with the inherent risk associated with the investment, compensate the investor enough, when compared to the definitive reduction in mortgage payments that result from early pay-down? And what happens if the mortgage is refinanced and interest rates rise? How do we account for such a possibility? It's futile to develop a model that encompasses these issues, because the answers implic-itly depend on an individual investor's attitudes toward risk and his or her need for security.

And there are other factors to consider, again dependent on an investor's personal situation. One consideration, of course, is that by using extra cash to reduce the mortgage, you are eliminating (or at least reducing) liquidity. Liquidity refers to the degree to which assets can easily be converted into cash. By paying down the mortgage instead of investing in a more liquid RRSP, you sacrifice a degree of liquidity. In an emergency, it's quite simple to cash an RRSP, notwith-standing the negative tax consequences of early redemption. It's far more difficult and undesirable to sell a house in an emergency.

Another consideration is the degree of diversification among different assets. Diversification, as we've seen, refers to the process of adding new investment instruments to a portfolio. And diversification is important; it raises the odds that when one asset decreases in value, another will increase, thereby negating the decrease. By paying down your mort-gage, you are effectively increasing the percentage of investment assets held in the "house" investment. Because investors typically have a large proportion of their invest-ments tied up in their house, most should probably work to decrease the level of that investment through diversifica-tion, by purchasing other investments.

Leverage

Now, let's turn to the related subject of investment leverage. It has three distinct faces — what I call the Good, the Bad, and the Ugly.

Leverage, in this context at least, simply means borrowing money to invest. The phenomenal stock market returns experienced in recent years tempted many investors into precisely that risky proposition. Unfortunately, if you succumbed to this strategy, the third quarter of 1998 probably taught you a lesson or two about the uglier side of leverage.

The basic arithmetic of leverage is simple and compelling. Suppose you have $10,000 invested in a mutual fund and the mutual fund goes up by 15% in one year. That means you've made $1,500 on your original $10,000 investment. Now, that's nice, but it could be a lot nicer. Because if you could somehow borrow an additional $10,000 (the equivalent of 100% leverage) and invest $20,000 ($10,000 + $10,000) in the mutual fund, you will have made a lot more by year's end.

With a 15% return, the $20,000 would become $23,000. Of course, from that amount you'd have to subtract the original loan of $10,000, plus any interest that you might have paid — say, $500 (5% on $10,000). That would leave you with $12,500. Wow! You started with $10,000 and turned it into $12,500, a full $1,000 more than if you had not borrowed. That's the equivalent of a 25% return. In other words, you've leveraged the fund's 15% return into a 25% return. That's what I call the Good.

Given the potential power of leverage, it's no wonder that people were rushing out to remortgage their homes, cottages, boats, and children to invest the proceeds in the stock market. As long as (after-tax) interest payments were lower than your earnings, you'd end up ahead of the game. In fact, if you borrowed $20,000 for every $10,000 you owned — a leverage factor of 200% — you could have earned 35% on your original $10,000 (and so on and so forth). The only constraint might have been a financial institution that placed restrictions on leverage or margining ratios — or perhaps a financial planner with some common sense.

So what went wrong?

Well, the arithmetic works in reverse as well. Yes, if markets move up by 15% a year, everything is peachy keen. But if markets suddenly drop 25% in one year (or worse, in one quarter), then you not only lose 25% on your original investment of $10,000, you lose 25% on the borrowed money as well. When it comes time to pay back the loan, the problems start to pile up.

For example, if you had borrowed $10,000 — for total assets of $20,000 — then a 25% loss wipes out $5,000 of your capital, leaving you with $15,000 at the end of the year. To add insult to injury, you must pay back the $10,000 loan, plus the (assumed) 5% interest. At year's end, therefore, your equity — your assets minus your liabilities — has dwindled to a mere $4,500. You original equity investment of $10,000 has lost 55% of its value, even though the market (fund, stock) only fell 25%. That's the Ugly side of leverage.

So, should you leverage? Is it a good idea? Will you make money? After all, in the long run, markets go up, don't they?

Well, by now you should know that there are no simple answers to these questions; all we can do is look at the odds.

Consistent with the theme of this book, we now ask the questions: What are the odds that you will benefit from leverage? What are the odds that you will regret exercising it?

First, let's take a good look at the upside. Let's say you are faced with a stock, mutual fund, or investment that is *expected* to earn 15% on average, in the long run. However, because there are no free lunches in the world, you have to contend with some risk. I assume that the volatility risk of this particular investment is 30%, which is a number I have used elsewhere in this book. So, facing this kind of investment, what happens if you leverage yourself?

You must pay particular attention to two factors — the leverage ratio and the borrowing (margin account) interest rate. Both will affect your outcome and the odds. The leverage ratio is the amount that you borrow to invest, expressed as a percentage of your original equity or capital. For example, if you have $10,000 and borrow $10,000, your leverage ratio is 100%. If you borrow only $5,000, your leverage ratio is 50%. If you don't borrow at all, your leverage ratio is 0%.

Next, the interest rate. This is simply the after-tax rate of interest that you'll be paying on the borrowed capital. In the present climate, the rate can range anywhere from 3% to 10%, depending on many considerations. The most important of these are your credit worthiness and the odds of your going bankrupt. Clearly, you want to borrow at the lowest possible interest rate, so that you get to keep as much of your market gains as possible.

Once you put the two factors together — leverage ratio and interest costs — you can do some intelligent analysis of how the leverage will affect your investments. (The numbers in the following three tables come from a computer simulation that estimates the probabilities of earning various return levels. See Chapters 8 and 9 for a more detailed discussion of how these computer simulations are performed.)

Table 7.2

Leverage: The Good
What are the Chances of Doubling the Market?

	Interest Cost		
	3%	5%	7%
Leverage Ratio			
0%	30.9%	30.9%	30.9%
25%	37.4%	36.9%	36.4%
50%	42.1%	41.2%	40.3%
100%	48.0%	46.7%	45.4%
250%	55.7%	53.8%	51.9%

Assumption: The market earns 15% on average and the volatility of the market is 30%.

Here's how to read Table 7.2. We'll assume that you are paying 5% interest on your margin account. If you leverage at a rate of 100% — one borrowed dollar for every dollar of original equity investment capital — then the odds of earning double the market rate (i.e., 2 x 15% = 30%) on your investment are 47%. In other words, the chances of converting $10,000 into $13,000 are 47%. That's slightly less than a one-in-two chance of doubling the market.

Compare that to the chances of earning the same 30% (2 x 15%) if you don't leverage at all. Table 7.1 states that the zero-leverage chances are a mere 31%. This is less than one chance in three. Notice the huge increase in the probability of doing very well — *if you leverage*. Sound tempting? Many have been lured.

Of course, as you can see from Table 7.2, if you have to pay more than 5% on your margin (borrowing) account, the odds of doing better than doubling the market will go down a bit. That's simply because the market has to earn even more — which is even less likely — in order to pay back your higher-interest borrowing. Likewise, if your interest cost is lower than 5%, your odds are somewhat better, but not by much. The real improvement in odds comes from higher amounts of leverage.

Look at the 250% leverage ratio case. Now, for the same doubling-the-market result, at a 5% margin, the numbers increase to 54%. This is a 54% chance (better than one in two) that you will earn more than a 30% return on your original investment. In fact, the higher your leverage ratio, the better your odds — up to a point. It's not surprising that so many have rushed to leverage their capital — the odds look so good.

Now, however, let's examine the Bad, the downside. What are the odds that you will lose money? What are the odds, with leverage, that you will end up with less than when you started?

Table 7.3

Leverage: The Bad
What are the Chances of Losing Money?

	Interest Cost		
	3%	**5%**	**7%**
Leverage Ratio			
0%	30.9%	30.9%	30.9%
25%	31.6%	32.0%	32.5%
50%	32.0%	32.8%	33.6%
100%	32.6%	33.8%	35.1%
250%	33.4%	35.2%	36.9%

Assumption: The market earns 15% on average and the volatility of the market is 30%.

Table 7.3 shows what happens when things go wrong. Although the odds of doubling the market are much greater for the leverage case, the odds of losing money are higher as well. For example, if you leverage yourself at 100% with a margin cost of 5%, the odds of losing money — i.e., the chances of having less than your original equity capital at year's end — are 34%.

Thus, if you start with $10,000 and borrow $10,000, at year's end, after paying back your loan with interest, the probability of having less than $10,000 is 34%.

Wait a minute. Thirty-four percent is not that much higher than the 31% chance of losing money if you don't use leverage at all. In other words, there's only a *3%* greater chance that using leverage will court disaster. That doesn't sound so bad, does it?

Is that the sum total of your risk?

Well, not exactly. Here's the Ugly.

To give you an indication of how ugly things can get with leverage, Table 7.4 provides the probability of losing a quarter of your initial investment from a leveraged transaction. The question is: What are the odds that if you start off

Table 7.4

Leverage: The Ugly
What are the Chances of Losing a Quarter of Your Initial Investment?

	Interest Cost		
	3%	**5%**	**7%**
Leverage Ratio			
0%	9.1%	9.1%	9.1%
25%	12.6%	12.9%	13.1%
50%	15.3%	15.9%	16.4%
100%	19.3%	20.2%	21.2%
250%	25.2%	26.8%	28.4%

Assumption: The market earns 15% on average and the volatility of the market is 30%.

with $10,000 — and borrow — you'll be left with less than $7,500 after 12 months? This would be a 25% loss of equity capital.

Well, if you don't leverage at all, the chances of suffering such a drastic reduction of capital are about 9%. But if you choose the 100% leverage route, and you pay a margin interest cost of 5%, your odds of losing a quarter of your initial investment are close to 20%. That's a one-in-five chance. Why are the odds so high? How can the odds of doing so poorly be so high? After all, the odds of doing very well were quite high as well. How can the odds be so high for both the Good and the Ugly?

Well, that's the key point with investment leverage. You are subjecting yourself to extremes. Things can go very well — or very badly. Very well if the market goes up; very badly if the market goes down. I like to say that leverage exaggerates both the severe upside and the severe downside.

On a technical level, you have increased the expected return of your investment, but you have increased the uncertainty as well. The higher uncertainty means that you are more likely to experience the extreme cases. In the good times, the extremes will be welcome. In the bad, they can bring you to the brink of bankruptcy.

CONCLUSION

In this chapter, we looked at two perennial questions related to borrowing and investing. First, we saw that there are several issues to consider when choosing between using extra cash to invest in an RRSP or to pay down a mortgage. The crucial consideration here is the amount of money you'd have at retirement following either of these strategies, using the model described in this chapter. The higher the expected return on investment, or the lower the mortgage rates, the more desirable investing in an RRSP will be. And given what I have said elsewhere in this book, you can in all likelihood expect to earn more on your RRSP than you will pay in interest on your mortgage. With that in mind, I conclude that, in strictly economic terms, you are better off keeping your mortgage as it is and contributing the maximum to your RRSP. But other factors, including your need for security, your tolerance for risk, and the importance of liquidity and diversification, must then be considered.

Next, we looked at whether using leverage — "borrowing to invest" in the purest sense — is a prudent strategy. Well, first of all, if your interest cost is tax-deductible, and market returns are treated as capital gains — deferred as long as you don't sell — then the upside of leverage can look quite appealing. By the same token, the downside is obvious. If things go wrong — and they certainly can — your loss is magnified. As Table 7.4 demonstrated, the odds of suffering a severe loss of your original equity are quite high.

Once again, I have reported the odds. Now, you must decide whether to take the umbrella.

Asset Allocation at Retirement: The Risk Is Not Enough

"Happy 65th birthday, Mr. Carlyle," sings the cheery voice at the other end of the telephone line. "It's now time to sell all your stocks and put the money in safe GICs, Canada Savings Bonds, and term deposits . . . After all, at your age, you can no longer afford to be taking that kind of risk."

I certainly hope you never receive such a ridiculous phone call — especially not on your 65th birthday. But the underlying assumption, that retirees can't afford to take financial risks, seems to be widespread among the investing public.

And it's precisely that assumption that I want to explore in this chapter. More specifically, I want to examine the interaction between age, investment, and financial risk. Ideally — by examining the odds — I would like to answer the following question: What is an appropriate asset allocation for retirees?

The issue has two cogently argued sides. On the one hand, because of your age, you *supposedly* have a short investment horizon ahead of you, and therefore lack the time needed to recover from any losses you might incur from owning a portfolio heavily weighted in equities. On the other hand, if you shift your investment assets to fixed-income products — especially when interest rates are mired at historically low levels — your earnings will decline, perhaps to the point of jeopardizing your standard of living.

Therefore, before I begin any discussion of investment strategies for retirees, you must determine the extent to which you are dependent on your financial assets to sustain your standard of living. Financial planners commonly refer to this as a "needs analysis."

What standard of living would you like to maintain during your retirement years? Do you want to travel the world? Will you stay at home? How expensive do you anticipate your lifestyle to be? These questions are probably not as easy to answer as it may seem. They certainly involve making many assumptions about your preferences and market prices. But the bottom line is that you — and only you — can estimate how much you'll require on an annual basis to maintain your desired standard of living in retirement. Ideally, this "needs analysis" should be conducted many years prior to retirement — so that you can better save for your goals. But at the very latest, you should do it at age 65.

Of course, if you qualify for any government or private pension, remember to subtract that amount from your annual needs. The objective is to get a desired number — an annual income level — that can be funded by your total financial assets. Without a good feel for what you will need, it's meaningless to talk about appropriate investments to finance those needs.

Once this first stage is out of the way, once you know — in current dollars — how much you will need every year in retirement, we can move on to stage two. There we discuss an appropriate asset allocation for your retirement years. But please bear in mind that we may have to revisit stage one — most likely to lower the desired annual income level — once you see how much money you'll need to comfortably support your anticipated standard of living. For the moment, however, let's maintain a positive attitude.

Now, at the risk of being considered a complete simpleton, I'd like to start this analysis by stating the obvious. If, at age 65, you have liquid financial assets that are 100 times greater than your anticipated needs (the annual consumption requirements), then no matter how you invest during your retirement years, you will never run out of money. Of course, very few Canadians are fortunate enough to be in this category. But presumably, those who are have no reason to change their investment philosophy at retirement.

Furthermore, at the risk of being considered coarse, if at age 65 you have liquid financial assets that are only five times greater than your desired annual income level, you are, quite frankly, doomed. If this is your situation, go back to stage one and rebudget. Or delay your retirement for a few more years. You certainly won't be able to invest your way out of this conundrum.

With these polar extremes out of the way, we are ready to address the question of an appropriate asset mix to support your desired annual consumption requirements. In other words, given your desired standard of living, what asset allocation — or mix between stocks, bonds, and bills — will minimize the probability that you will run out of money during your retirement years? A little later in this chapter, I will flip the question around and ask the exact opposite: What is a sustainable real standard of living, given a particular wealth level?

So without further ado, let's look at some hypothetical numbers.

You've just retired at age 65 with a fairly decent pension, which should provide a large portion of your needs on an annual basis. In addition — after many years of contributing to an RRSP — you've managed to build a nest egg of approximately $200,000, which is currently sitting in an assortment of mutual funds, GICs, and other minor investments that you don't much care for. Your house, fortunately, is fully paid for, and you have no other major liabilities.

After conducting a needs analysis, taking full account of your lifestyle choices and retirement plans, you've determined that you require — in addition to your pension — approximately $7,500 each and every year until the end of your life. Naturally, you hope that your RRSP will be able to provide this additional amount.

Before we continue, I should clarify what is meant by $7,500 per year. This estimate assumes that today's prices — on which you based your needs — will remain the same throughout your retirement. In other words, it assumes that the inflation rate for goods and services will be zero for the next 30 years. Rather unrealistic, I'm sure you'd agree. True, inflation has averaged only 2% to 3% over the last few years. But there is no guarantee — always a positive probability — that the rate cannot or will not increase. Indeed, economic history teaches us that price inflation can resurface suddenly and dramatically. Furthermore, the projected inflation rate for retirees may in fact be higher than the general inflation rate for the population at large. Think of geriatric medical care and its costs over the years.

Therefore, a better way to deal with long-term planning (given inflation uncertainty) is to budget and state your needs in real, *after-inflation* terms. At the same time, you must also project your investment returns in real, after-inflation terms. Let me explain. As I said earlier, you essentially want to consume $7,500 *1999 dollars* for the rest of your life. By real consumption, I mean that you will consume $7,500 in your 65th year, $7,500 multiplied by the first year's inflation rate in your 66th year, $7,500 multiplied by the first and second years' inflation rate in your 67th year, and so on. However, to keep things in balance, when I talk about what your money can earn, I will look at returns in after-inflation terms, to account for the fact that your needs were expressed in the same framework.

Ideally, your pension plan comes with some form of inflation protection — or indexing — as well. (Ask about it.) The indexing can be implicitly tied to the consumer price index (CPI), or implicitly tied to the performance of some investment fund.

Practically speaking, the easiest way to get at the $7,500 you'll need each year — about $625 per month — is to set up a systematic withdrawal plan that sells an appropriate number of stocks, mutual funds, or bonds each month, to create the desired cash flow. This is like a reverse dollar-cost averaging strategy. Instead of *buying* an arbitrary number of units with a fixed amount of cash each month, you are *selling* an arbitrary number of units to create a fixed amount of revenue each month. Then, to account for any price inflation in your consumption needs, you increase the amount withdrawn under the systematic plan on a yearly basis.

Now, before we proceed, we must deal with one other unpleasant aspect of financial budgeting for retirement — income taxes.

The $7,500 that you need each year probably does not account for income taxes. So if you are planning to consume $7,500 from your nest egg each year, you will probably have to withdraw more than that, because of the income taxes that will be due. Everything you pull out of an RRSP or RRIF will be taxed at your marginal tax bracket because you have never actually paid income tax on that money. Remember, those funds were deducted from income in the year that you made your RRSP contribution.

What this all boils down to is that if you need $7,500 to live on — and you're in the 50% marginal income tax bracket, for example — then you will really have to withdraw $15,000 from the nest egg. Half of it — the 50% tax — will go to Ottawa (and back, very indirectly, to you, taking the optimistic and patriotic view); the other half you will be able to consume yourself. Yes, it sounds a bit depressing and drastic. But consider the bright side: you have never paid any income tax on that money, and it has grown, tax-deferred, for all those years.

Now, a Pandora's box that I would certainly like to avoid is the whole question of what your marginal tax bracket will be 10 or 20 years from now. Today, we know that the highest Canadian marginal tax bracket is in the 50% to 55% range. But who's to say that provincial and federal authorities won't raise that number, especially as it applies to funds withdrawn from an RRSP or RRIF? In fact, on a professional level, I feel much more confident predicting the long-term expected rate of return from various asset classes than I do predicting what the income tax structure will look like in 15 years. We might move toward a flatter tax system, in which all income is taxed at roughly the same rate; or we may see an increase in progressivity, which would raise tax rates on the wealthiest above the current 50% to 55% region. Unfortunately, I can't give you the odds on this one, and it's probably one of the biggest question marks in the financial planning equation. Nevertheless, we must play the game of life based on the current rules, and we must therefore make plans based on the current tax system.

Let me, then, recap what we have done. By this point, you should have a pretty good sense of your needs, and those needs should be specified on a pre-tax basis. In the example we've been using, you have $200,000 in an RRSP, and will need to consume or withdraw $15,000, in after-inflation, pre-tax terms.

Roughly speaking, therefore, your Needs-to-Wealth (abbreviated as NtW) ratio is $15,000/$200,000 = 7.5%. Another way of looking at it is to say that your annual income needs represent 7.5% of the initial wealth available to support those needs. Thus, if you had $400,000 in an RRSP and your needs were $30,000, you would also have a 7.5% Needs-to-Wealth ratio. This ratio is important because it gives you a general sense of what kind of investment returns you'll require to support your annual needs. I would argue that all people — at age 65 — with a 7.5% NtW ratio are more or less in the same boat. That's because whether they have $1,000,000 or a mere $100,000 at retirement, they all have the same relative needs.

We are now ready to revisit the main question. Is $200,000 enough to support your $15,000 annual needs? The answer, of course, really depends on what you do with — or how you invest — the $200,000. Another way of asking the question is, can you sustain a NtW ratio of 7.5%? The answer to this question clearly depends on your asset allocation. It depends on what your investment portfolio looks like during your retirement years.

First of all, let's see if you'll be able to live on interest and dividends alone. Evidently, the $200,000 will have to generate exactly 7.5% in order to create $15,000 — after inflation and before taxes. Unfortunately, GICs, Canada Savings Bonds, and money market funds will earn you nowhere near that amount. So you have a clear choice: you can invest in these relatively safe investments, knowing that eventually you will have to encroach on your capital and may run out of money; or you can invest a bit more aggressively, and hopefully build your capital. (Or, of course, you can always decide to reduce consumption.)

The math is relatively simple. If your money earns a fixed 5% in real terms, and you insist on consuming $15,000 each and every year, you will run out of money in precisely 22 years. That's because the present value of $15,000, discounted at the rate of 5%, is exactly equal to $200,000. Stated differently, a $200,000 mortgage, amortized at a rate of 5%, will be paid off in exactly 22 years, when the annual payments add up to $15,000.

Okay, you say to yourself, if I can earn a consistent 5% every year — in real terms — my money will last for exactly 22 years. That's plenty of time, no?

Well, maybe, or maybe not. Statistics tell us that a male — at age 65 — has a 30% chance of living for 22 more years; a female has a 48% chance of living for 22 more years (we'll discuss this in some detail in Chapter 9 when we look at mortality tables). So let's put two and two together and see what happens.

If you earn 5%, you'll run out of money in 22 years. That much is clear. But there's a 30% chance (48% for women) of living for 22 more years. In other words, there is a 30% (48%) chance of *outliving your money*, if you earn 5% each and every year. Why? Well, the odds of outliving your money are the odds of being alive when the money runs out. If you know exactly when the money will run out, and you know the odds of living to that point, put them together and you have the odds of outliving your money.

Similarly, if your $200,000 nest egg earns a fixed 4% in real terms, you will run out of money even sooner — in exactly 19 years — because you are earning less. And the odds of living for 19 more years are, not surprisingly, higher than the odds of living for 22 more years. The chances are 42% for males and 60% for females. So if you earn 4% each and every year, the odds of running out of money are 42% and 60% respectively.

Another way of saying this is that slightly more than two

of every five men (and three of every five women) will out-live $200,000 invested at 4%, if their annual pre-tax needs are $15,000.

I trust this procedure is clear. Simply compute when the money will run out, then look at the probability of being alive at that time. The higher the number, the more likely it is that your standard of living is simply not sustainable. At some point, you will have to reduce your withdrawals, or recalculate your needs, to avoid starvation.

The same formula applies in the other direction. If your capital can earn 6% in real terms, you won't run out of money for 27 years. For a 65-year-old, 27 years may seem pretty far out in the future. Indeed, the male at that age has only a 14% chance of living that much longer (and running out of money); women have a 28% chance. These figures are low, but not entirely comforting, especially for the female.

Finally, if you are lucky or smart enough to have your capital earn 7.5% each year — you'll notice it works out to $15,000 each year — you will *never run out of money*. Another way to think of this is that a $200,000 mortgage, amortized at 7.5%, with annual payments of $15,000, will never be paid off. You will barely manage to pay the interest, let alone pay down the principal.

So what are the odds of running out of money when your capital earns 7.5% each and every year? Well, I hope you see that they are zero for both males and females. In fact, even if you earned slightly less — 7.25% each year — you would run out of money in exactly 45 years. And the odds of being alive then are zero for both males and females as well.

No great secrets here, then: the less you earn, on an annual basis, the sooner your money will run out, assuming that you'll need $15,000 in real terms each year. Incidentally, all of these calculations — though somewhat beyond the scope of this book — can be easily performed with the aid of a calculator or spreadsheet, and then you can examine the odds from a mortality table. This calculation is essentially a mortgage amortization schedule that tells you when the money will run out — as opposed to when the mortgage will be paid off.

Table 8.1 puts a different spin on mortality statistics by looking at when your money will run out, and then stating the probability of living to that age.

Table 8.1

The Probability of Starvation If You Run Out of Money at Various Ages

(Current age is 65)		
Age	Female	Male
70	94.0%	89.2%
75	85.5%	75.1%
80	73.4%	57.6%
85	56.6%	38.2%
90	35.9%	20.1%
95	18.6%	7.5%

(Source: Statistics Canada 1996; see also Appendix)

What does this chart reveal? Well, for one thing, it tell us that if (at age 65) your financial plan is only valid for 20 years (age 85), there's a 56% chance for females (38% for males) that you'll still be alive when you run out of money. This is the probability of outliving wealth. It is the probability of still being alive when there is no more money in the account.

Now, at some point, of course, such a poor soul would realize that he or she is about to run out of money and would lower their annual consumption, and never really starve. In fact, you might be thinking, social support payments would kick in long before disaster struck. Or your children might be able to lend financial support. Nobody, in other words, really starves.

Absolutely. I agree wholeheartedly; nobody would actually reach starvation. Certainly, nobody would withdraw that final year's sum of $15,000 and then say, "Oops, what do I do next year?" But the idea is to plan ahead and to realize the consequences of your actions in their most drastic, worst-case forms. To avert a potential crisis — *now* — you must do one of two things: (a) invest more aggressively, so that you earn more return on your nest egg, or (b) cut down on your consumption — in other words, reduce your needs.

But here is the $200,000 question. What if you don't know exactly what your rate of return will be? Sure, with perfect foresight of investment returns, you would know precisely when the money would run out and you could then talk about the chances of living to that point. But in fact, nobody can know with utter certainty when his or her money will run out, because nobody can know with utter certainty what the annual rate of return will be. So how can we perform this exercise in the real world, where market returns fluctuate on a day-to-day basis?

Well, here is where the probabilities come in again. We are now ready for the full-fledged model. I call it the dual uncertainty model because there are really two probabilities that you have to concern yourself with — the investment probabilities and the mortality probabilities. These are the two sources of uncertainty that must be dealt with here.

So we are going to work with two sources of randomness. The first is the odds of earning a particular rate of return. The second is the odds of living to a particular age. Clearly, the odds of earning a specific return depend on your asset allocation — that is, on how you divide your capital between stocks, bonds, and other investments — and we will account for that explicitly. We will look at the odds, depending on how aggressively you decide to invest.

The technical question I want to investigate is: What

asset allocation would maximize the probability that you will be able to consume $7,500 annually for the rest of your life?

Before I get into a full-throttle explanation, here is a sample table.

Table 8.2

Probability of Outliving Your Money — Depending on Asset Allocation

(Current age is 65; initial wealth is $200,000; annual real withdrawal is $15,000; NtW Ratio is 7.5%)

Equity Allocation*	Male	Female
0%	47%	71%
20%	37%	59%
40%	30%	47%
60%	26%	39%
80%	23%	35%
100%	22%	32%

The remaining wealth, that portion not allocated to the equity market, is invested in short-term GICs or money market funds.

What does this table tell us? It tells us, for example, that if a 65-year-old female allocates all of her $200,000 to short-term GICs or money market funds, and has zero exposure to the equity markets, there is a 71% chance that she will not be able to consume the desired $15,000. In other words, with a real consumption level of $15,000, there's a 71% chance that she will outlive her money. In contrast, a 65-year-old male who allocates 0% to equities will have a 47% chance of outliving his money. This number is still quite high, but as you probably guessed, it's lower than the female's probability because men don't usually live — and consume — as long as women.

Now, what happens if you invest in — or allocate your assets to — funds with somewhat greater variability, but higher long-term growth rates? The fluctuations may hurt in the short term, but what do the overall odds look like when you take account of mortality and investment risk?

The answers are contained in the table. As the 65-year-old moves into a more aggressive allocation to equity, the probability of outliving wealth, surprisingly, decreases. For example, with a 60% allocation to equity, women have a 39% chance of running out of money; men have a 26% chance.

The higher average long-term rate of return counteracts the effects of the equity investment's short-term volatility, yielding lower "starvation odds."

Your question at this point, of course, is how and where did I come up with these numbers?

I'm glad you asked.

I borrowed a technique developed by scientists over the last few decades to deal with complicated questions in nuclear physics. These days, it's used in everything from traffic control to designing better soap. And it's called the method of Monte Carlo simulation. We used this method in earlier chapters; now let me explain how it works in more detail.

Together with some colleagues at York University, I constructed a computer program that generates millions of different scenarios for the financial markets and human mortality. It is, if you like, the ultimate imagination machine. In one scenario you live to the ripe old age of 95; in another scenario you live to age 75. Some scenarios show the stock market booming for the next 20 years; others indicate a 10-year bear market. The probabilities — or relative occurrences — for these human life-span scenarios are taken from Statistics Canada mortality tables; the probabilities for stock market and interest-rate evolution are generated using historical statistical estimates.

As you probably know, simulations of future market behaviour have been employed quite successfully in corporate risk management, when a company wants to compute the probability of losing a specific amount of money over a particular time horizon. Government regulators also use the Monte Carlo method to estimate and measure the stability of the financial system.

As you might have guessed, the name Monte Carlo itself comes from the underlying roulette wheel in the computer that generates the different scenarios. It may sound a bit removed to let a computer determine what the future will look like. But in fact, with its exhaustive search ability, it does cover all possible contingencies, every possible scenario of what could happen over the next 40 years.

True, no computer could have predicted the collapse of the Asian economies, or the debt default of the Russian government. The point is not to identify or predict *specific* events; rather, it is to compute all possibilities for the evolution of the financial markets in conjunction with human mortality.

In one scenario, the computer predicted that the Canadian stock market would fall by 25% in one quarter. The computer certainly didn't give a reason. It didn't explain *why* that would happen. It simply said that it was within the realm of possibility. And lo and behold, during the third quarter of 1998, the TSE300 index fell by roughly that amount. Quite uncanny!

Obviously, this doesn't mean that the computer actually predicted the future. It simply means that, using the Monte Carlo simulation, it computed a remote possibility of the market's declining by 25% in one quarter — and, implicitly, recommended that we should plan for such a possibility. I don't want to alarm you unnecessarily, but in a few scenarios it generated drops even scarier than 25%; fortunately, the computer estimated the odds of such events to be very small.

Now comes the fun part. After leaving the computer on

all night, running millions of these future scenarios, we returned in the morning and started counting.

Specifically, for each and every possible asset allocation, we counted the number of times that the 65-year-old who consumes $15,000 per year will run out of money before he or she dies. These are the people who starve. The remaining people, who die with wealth, have managed to avoid outliving their money. The ratio of the former to the latter provides us with the probability of outliving your money. We then sift through the cases to locate the asset allocation that minimizes the probability of outliving wealth.

Let's look at an example. In one simulation, a 65-year-old woman who invested all of her capital in the stock market — consuming $15,000 real dollars each year — ran out of money in roughly five years because she had the uncanny bad luck of investing right before a horrendous (computer-generated) bear market. Again, however, the computer assigned a very low probability to this event.

In another scenario, we found that a 45-year-old male was able to take (very) early retirement, with only $200,000 in wealth, and still manage to consume $15,000 per year for life, by investing completely in equities. But this is because the computer killed him off at age 68, long before his full life expectancy. (I think it was a skydiving accident.) The computer also assigned this event — a robust stock market combined with early death — a very low probability. Overall, the chance that a 45-year-old man will be able to retire at age 45, with only $200,000 to support a spending habit of $15,000 per year, is not great.

Before I go further, I must emphasize the assumptions that go into such a Monte Carlo simulation study. First, as I mentioned, I assumed that future human longevity patterns would obey the above-mentioned mortality tables published by Statistics Canada in 1996.

If you believe that you are healthier than the average

Canadian — and that these numbers do not apply to you —
then your probabilities of outliving your wealth are even
higher than the above estimates. Remember, if you live
longer, you consume longer, which — all else being equal
— increases the odds of starvation.

Second, I assumed that the real — after-inflation — rate
of return from short-term cash in GICs, or money market
funds, would be 1.5% per annum. Yes, I know that the current rate on bank GICs is closer to 4%. But keep in mind
that the inflation rate is between 1% and 2%, and we are
concerned here with real — after-inflation — returns. So
projecting ahead, a 1.5% return does not sound unreason-
ably conservative. Indeed, if you strongly believe that you
can earn more than that — in real terms — without incurring any market volatility risk, then your probability of
outliving wealth and running out of money will be lower.

Third, I assumed that the long-term real rate of return
from the equity markets would be 7.5%, with a volatility of
16.5%. I am not assuming that you will earn 7.5% in real
terms each year. Rather, I'm assuming that in the long term,
you'll earn *an average of 7.5% per annum*, with a volatility
of 16.5%. (Remember that volatility is a measure of how
wide the spectrum of investment returns is expected to be.
A volatility number of 20% means that 95% of the time, the
returns will be within 2 x 20% = 40% of the expected value.)
The nominal, pre-inflation, 25%–30% returns that North
American markets have experienced in recent years cannot
persist in the long run. In fact, even 7.5% may be a bit aggressive, given that the Canadian stock market has only managed
to earn about 5% annually in real terms since 1957.

Fourth, I assumed that you would be able to diversify
internationally by at least 36%, if not more. Within an RRSP
— with a current 20% restriction on foreign content — the
36% can be achieved by investing 20% directly into a foreign-content mutual fund, and the other 80% into a mutual

fund that invests another 20% in foreign content. The original 20% plus the secondary investment (20% of 80%) yields exactly 36%.

Finally, don't forget transaction costs. I very much doubt that you can earn 7.5% in real terms by investing in an equity fund with a management expense ratio (MER) of 3%. Low MERs are crucial.

Now, obviously, the age (65) and NtW ratio (7.5%) may not apply to your precise situation. So let's examine the odds for age 75, with the same NtW ratio of 7.5%. In this case, you are 75 years old, have nest-egg capital of $200,000, and want to withdraw $15,000 every year.

Table 8.3

Probability of Outliving Your Money — Depending on Asset Allocation

(Current age is 75; initial wealth is $200,000; annual real withdrawal is $15,000; NtW Ratio is 7.5%)

Equity Allocation*	Male	Female
0%	17%	29%
20%	13%	23%
40%	11%	19%
60%	10%	16%
80%	9%	15%
100%	9%	15%

The remaining wealth, the portion not allocated to the equity market, is invested in short-term GICs or money market funds.

A few things should be immediately evident from Table 8.3. First, the probability of outliving wealth is uniformly lower at all asset allocation levels. For men, the "starvation probability" numbers range from 17% to 9%, much lower (and much better) than the 47% to 22% range we had for a 65-year-old in the same situation. The reason is quite simple: you are 10 years older and therefore have 10 fewer years of consumption ahead of you. The odds of outliving your money, therefore, *must* be lower.

The same applies for the 75-year-old woman; her numbers now range from 29% to 15%. That's higher than it is for men because she lives longer. But they, too, are lower than the same numbers for a comparable 65-year-old female, which were 71% to 32%.

Another interesting thing to note about Table 8.3 is that the numbers level off at a 40% allocation to equity. In other words, any *additional* allocation doesn't do much to reduce the probability of shortfall or starvation. Why is this? Shouldn't higher levels of equity continue to reduce the starvation numbers? Well, the fact is that higher equity allocations *will* increase the growth rate of your portfolio in the long run. But in the short run, there's always some risk of a bad run of luck. Stated differently, with a 100% allocation to equities, there's a 9% to 15% chance that in the first few years you will experience negative returns, thus causing an erosion of capital from which you cannot recuperate in time.

To give a sense of the richness of the Monte Carlo approach, here's another collection of simulated scenarios. This time, we looked at a 55-year-old, perhaps interested in early retirement.

From Table 8.4, we can see that a female who consumes $15,000 every year from an original nest egg of $200,000 has a 96% chance of outliving her wealth — if all of the money is invested in short-term GICs or money market funds. Essentially, with that kind of a low-volatility (and low-return) asset allocation, there is no hope for an early retirement. At the other extreme, with a 100% allocation to equities, the odds of starvation are cut in half. As you can see, the probability of outliving wealth is reduced to 48% with a complete allocation to the equity market. Granted, a 48% chance of starvation is still rather intimidating, and not tolerable by any means. But the dramatic reduction from 96% to 48% is persuasive, and yields insight into the power of long-term equity growth, despite the associated volatility.

Table 8.4

Probability of Outliving Your Money — Depending on Asset Allocation

(Current age is 55; initial wealth is $200,000; annual real withdrawal is $15,000; NtW Ratio is 7.5%)

Equity Allocation*	Male	Female
0%	83%	96%
20%	72%	90%
40%	59%	78%
60%	48%	63%
80%	42%	54%
100%	38%	48%

The remaining wealth, the portion not allocated to the equity market, is invested in short-term GICs or money market funds.

The male numbers are lower — remember, males don't live as long and therefore consume less — but the odds are still quite high. The male starvation numbers range from 83% to 38% — not a very reliable way to retire. The message, however, remains the same: The best odds come from a higher allocation to the (volatile) risky asset class.

In sum, I would conclude that — especially for women — early retirement at age 55, with a 7.5% Needs-to-Wealth ratio, is unsustainable no matter how you allocate the funds.

But what if you take early retirement and consume less than $15,000 per year from your $200,000 nest egg? In other words, what if your Needs-to-Wealth ratio is lower? Intuitively, you would expect to be better off, in the sense that your odds should look better. Well, Table 8.5 confirms this intuition and gives us some precise results. Here, I am using the same type of computer simulation, but assuming that you are consuming only $10,000 per year from your $200,000 nest egg. Now, the NtW ratio is 5%.

Table 8.5

Probability of Outliving Your Money — Depending on Asset Allocation

(Current age is 55; initial wealth is $200,000; annual real withdrawal is $10,000; NtW Ratio is 5.0%)

Equity Allocation*	Male	Female
0%	40%	63%
20%	26%	42%
40%	18%	28%
60%	15%	21%
80%	14%	19%
100%	13%	18%

The remaining wealth, the portion not allocated to the equity market, is invested in short-term GICs or money market funds.

Indeed, Table 8.5 shows odds that are uniformly lower than Table 8.4, because the annual consumption level is much lower. For example, a woman with zero allocation to the equity markets now has a 63% chance of outliving her wealth, which is significantly less than the 96% chance attached to $15,000 of consumption. Yes, 63% is still high, but if she turns to higher equity allocations, the numbers decline substantially. In fact, a 100% allocation to equity leads to an 18% chance of starvation — less than one in five.

The male story is similar. A complete allocation to short-term GICs or money market funds yields a 40% chance of starvation. Higher allocations to equities will reduce those numbers, until the probability of starvation reaches 13% at total equity exposure. Once again, the male fares better than the female, given the same consumption numbers.

The message about early retirement should be fairly clear.

A Needs-to-Wealth ratio of 7.5% — or higher — is *probably not sustainable with any equity allocation.* A much lower NtW ratio of 5%, combined with a substantial allocation to the equity markets, gives you fairly reasonable odds.

This raises an important question: What is an acceptable starvation probability? Is 10% to 15% too high? If — according to Table 8.2 — the lowest level a 65-year-old can achieve is 22% for men and 32% for women, it still seems that the $15,000 real-dollar annual spending plan, based on $200,000 initial wealth, is not very sustainable, no matter what he or she does. Yes, a total allocation to GIC-type instruments will make it much worse — 47% and 71% respectively, but that is hardly reassuring. So what else can be done?

The answer is twofold. First, you will probably have to revisit stage one, recompute, and probably reduce your needs. Second, you will have to diversify across more than just equity-based investments and simple GICs. You'll need other asset classes — government and corporate bonds are just one example.

Let's look at the question in another way. Instead of starting with a desired annual amount — $15,000 in our earlier example — let's examine what a reasonable withdrawal rate would be. What *is* a sustainable standard of living? And what asset allocation will maximize the income you can extract each year?

A Different Perspective

So let's start over. You have just retired at age 65 with a decent pension and an additional $100,000 in tax-sheltered savings. (If you have more capital, $200,000 for example, you scale things up by two, or vice versa if you have less.) You approach your financial planner with an innocent-sounding question. Instead of doing the needs analysis and pre-specifying a desired annual level of consumption, you flip it around. You ask: "How much can I afford to withdraw from the $100,000 on an annual basis in real — after-inflation — terms, for the rest of my life? What real standard of living can I afford? Is $10,000, inflation-adjusted, too high? Is $3,000 too low?"

As you may have noticed, the popular financial planning software packages — the textbook solution to this classic problem — makes two crucial and unrealistic assumptions. They are: (a) how long a 65-year-old female will live and (b) the long-term average real rate of return — net of inflation — on investment. For example, if you assume that you will live for 15 more years, and your money will earn a real 6% per year for the rest of your life, then any respectable financial software package will tell you that the present value of $10,000 is exactly $100,000. Thus, a lifetime standard of living of $10,000 per year, in real terms, is exactly sustainable from an initial sum of $100,000 — *if you know with perfect certainty that you will live for only 15 more years.*

As I argued earlier, a longer assumed period in retirement, together with a lower assumed real rate of return, will result in a lower sustainable consumption. In contrast, a shorter assumed period in retirement, together with a higher assumed real rate of return, will result in a higher sustainable consumption.

But enough of textbook cases. What happens in real life?

In real life, the length of one's life is random. And so is the real rate of return. How can we simply assume something that by nature is random? How can we deal with this dual uncertainty? Can we quantify the risk? What are the odds?

Once again, the answer to this question depends on the asset allocation of the individual in question. Chances are that a more conservative asset allocation will result in a lower sustainable lifetime annual consumption rate (SLACR).

A more aggressive asset allocation will result in a higher SLACR.

Tables 8.6 and 8.7 provide a rough estimate of the relationship between asset allocation and real sustainable lifetime annual consumption rates for males and females aged 65.

Here's one example. If a 65-year-old female allocates all of her $100,000 to GICs, Canada Savings Bonds, and money market funds (what we call risk-free investments), then, with 90% certainty, the sustainable lifetime annual consumption rate is an inflation-adjusted $3,836. Not a lot of money, I'm sure you'll agree.

If she consumes any more than $3,836 in real terms, given a complete allocation to GICs, CSBs, etc., she will incur a shortfall at some point in her life — with 10% certainty. In other words, there's at least a 10% chance that her money will run out while she's still alive. On the other hand, if she's willing to make a 60% allocation to equity and a 40% allocation to bonds, she can actually afford to consume an inflation-adjusted $5,168 per year for the rest of her life. This more generous standard of living is also sustainable with 90% certainty.

Overall, these numbers may seem low. But remember that they are in real terms, also known as 1999 dollars. In 10 years' time, the woman will be consuming much more than $5,168 in nominal terms, but it will still be worth $5,168 in 1999 dollars.

Now, you may ask yourself, how can she consume more, and still maintain the same odds of sustainability? The answer, of course, lies in the long-term growth of equities, compared with GICs, CSBs, and money market funds. True, there is a short-term risk in investing in equities. But the probability of long-term sustainability remains 90%. As I have mentioned in many contexts in this book, the risk of equities pays off.

Tables 8.6 and 8.7 display the sustainable lifetime annual consumption rate as a function of — or depending on — the percentage allocation to stocks and bonds. Specifically, the left-hand column in both tables represents the allocation to bonds — denoted by the letter B. The top row in both tables represents the allocation to equity — denoted by the letter E. So, for example, the coordinates B = 40%

Table 8.6

What Is Your 90% SLACR — Depending on Allocation of Assets Between Bonds (Vertical) and Equity (Horizontal?)*

(65-year-old male; $100,000 initial wealth)

B\E	0%	20%	40%	60%	80%	100%
0%	$4,419	$4,970	$5,368	$5,601	$5,680	$5,624
20%	$4,586	$5,134	$5,525	$5,749	$5,806	
40%	$4,676	$5,214	$5,596	$5,812		
60%	$4,688	$5,212	$5,583			
80%	$4,628	$5,134				
100%	$4,506					

Table 8.7

What is Your 90% SLACR?

(65-year-old female; $100,000 initial wealth)

B\E	0%	20%	40%	60%	80%	100%
0%	$3,836	$4,386	$4,767	$4,969	$5,015	$4,934
20%	$4,001	$4,549	$4,921	$5,114	$5,149	
40%	$4,079	$4,616	$4,980	$5,168		
60%	$4,074	$4,594	$4,950			
80%	$3,995	$4,494				
100%	$3,856					

*Assumptions: The remainder of capital earns the risk-free rate. In real terms, the risk-free rate of return is 1.5%. The return on bonds is 3.5%, with a volatility of 11.5%. The return on equity is 7.5%, with a volatility of 16.5%. Correlation between bonds and equity is 10%. (Source: Statistics Canada 1996 mortality projections.)

and E = 40% mean that 40% has been allocated to bonds, 40% has been allocated to equities, and the remaining 20% has been allocated to short-term cash, GICs, or money market funds.

Search the tables for the highest dollar amount. Its coordinates are the ones that will lead to the highest possible annual consumption rate — with 90% probability.

The male, as you can see, eats more (as usual). The probability of living to any particular age is lower for males than it is for females. Consequently, men can afford to consume more, and still maintain the same 90% chance of not running out of money. At the point of complete allocation to GICs, CSBs, and money market funds, the male can afford to consume an inflation-adjusted $4,419. Likewise, with a 60% allocation to equity and 40% allocation to bonds, he can afford to consume an inflation-adjusted $5,812 per year for the rest of his life.

How did we get these numbers?

Once again, it was the Monte Carlo simulation. We generated millions of scenarios for consumption, asset allocation, and human mortality, and then looked for the cases where the probability of starvation was less than 10% — i.e., a probability of sustainability that was greater than 90%.

CONCLUSION

At the risk of losing the forest for the trees, let me try to summarize what the main points are — and what they are not.

First, there is nothing magical about age 65 as it pertains to asset allocation, exposure to risk, and equity-based mutual funds. At age 65, you can expect to live more than 20 years, a time horizon long enough for an exposure to equity. The odds are that you will minimize the probability of starvation with a high allocation to equity, not with GICs and money market funds. In fact, we saw that a 65-year-old woman who needs to withdraw a fixed annual amount — in our example, 7.5% of her initial wealth — will lower her probability of shortfall from 71% to 32% by assuming more stock market and equity-based risk. The numbers drop dramatically when you go from 0% equity to 50% equity, but start to decline with even higher levels of equity allocation. The male experiences a similar reduction, from 47% to 22%.

From the point of view of pure odds, then, it is very important to have some exposure to equity-based investments, even during your retirement years.

The question, as always, is how much exposure? What is appropriate for you?

At this point, I must excuse myself and refer you to your licensed financial planner, broker, or investment adviser. No, I am not being lazy or coy.

Indeed, when *I* am contemplating a personal asset-allocation decision, I try to find the course of action that will maximize the probability of success. But there are so many more aspects to *your* financial life, such as taxes, estates, insurance, debts, and pensions, that I could not possibly provide you with a one-size-fits-all table, with a universal answer to all your asset allocation questions.

My objective is much more modest. It's an attempt to make you *think* differently about your retirement asset allocation. In fact, if there's one thing you remember from this chapter, I hope it's the following.

When you get financial retirement advice, always be prepared to ask: "What are the odds that I will outlive my money, if I follow your suggestions?" If the answer is simply too high for your comfort level, change the plan, or change the planner.

May you live long, and prosper!

Your RRSP Saving Years Are Over: So What's Next?

By any measure, the Registered Retirement Savings Plan (RRSP) has long been the single most important element of financial planning in Canada. Taking advantage of its major benefits — an immediate tax deduction and tax-sheltered growth — Canadians have enthusiastically embraced the RRSP as a smart and prudent financial tool. An annual avalanche of marketing material helps confirm them in this conviction.

Yet relatively little thought is paid to the eventual payout of RRSP funds at retirement and the financial options that are available. In fact, the Canadian Association of Retired Persons (CARP) estimates that approximately 150,000–200,000 people are required to make an RRSP conversion decision each year.

What exactly are their choices? The Income Tax Act now stipulates that at retirement (to be specific, by age 69), all Canadians must do one of the following:

1. withdraw the funds from the RRSP;
2. convert the RRSP to a Registered Retirement Income Fund (RRIF); or
3. purchase an annuity from an insurance company.

If you choose option 1, and simply cash in the RRSP, its proceeds are fully taxable. That means, for example, that if you have $100,000 in your RRSP fund and collapse it, you will pay income tax on the entire amount in the single year. Obviously, unless there are very compelling reasons for doing so, this is not a strategy I would ordinarily recommend.

The other two options, on the other hand — converting to a RRIF or buying a life annuity — will preserve the tax-sheltered status of your retirement nest egg.

It's important to remember that the RRIF and the annuity are not at all the same. They are two entirely different methods of financing retirement, each having different characteristics and implications. Naturally, therefore, the decision to choose one over the other should be made with extreme caution.

That is especially the case because, although the RRIF decision is reversible, the purchase of a life annuity is not. Once you've signed the papers, you're committed to that course — for better or worse.

In fact, the general question of whether or not to annuitize applies to many people at age 65 who are about to retire and face the choice of taking the funds out of the company pension plan or annuitizing the proceeds. With that in mind, from here on I will use age 65 as the base example; however, the general idea applies equally to age 69.

This annuity question is so important, and affects so many people, that I have made it the primary focus of this chapter. In Chapter 8, we focused on the general question of an appropriate asset allocation to maintain during your retirement years. Here, I will look at how you go about liquidating those assets, with particular emphasis on how annuities work and when is the best time to buy one.

At this point, let me state my own view: Unless there are extenuating circumstances, at retirement, it makes very little sense for males under the age of 75 or females under the age of 80 to purchase life annuities or to annuitize any additional non-pension wealth.

There are two exceptions to this general rule, although both are rare. One is a situation in which long-term interest rates are extraordinarily high. The second may occur if consumers have solid reasons to believe that they are much healthier than average. You may have heard similar advice from other financial planners and commentators, but my objective is to explain and justify this fact by — as you guessed it — carefully examining the odds.

Before we delve further into the subject of how to manage your post-retirement financial affairs, it's important to spend a little time understanding mortality tables and to get a sense of how long people are living and spending in retirement. In the previous chapter, you saw how life expectancies affect investment decisions. Here, I'll briefly show you related data that will help you interpret how much money you can expect to receive from a life annuity at various ages.

How Long Do We Live?

The median life span of Canadian males in 1996 was approximately 78.6 years at birth; for females, it was 84.3 years at birth. But what exactly does this mean? Does it mean that if you are a retired 75-year-old male (or female), you can expect to live only 3.6 (or 9.3) more years in retirement? Does it mean that if you are 78 years old, you can expect to live another six months (or six years)?

Of course, the answer to both questions is a resounding no.

The key qualifier here is that the median life span only applies *at birth*. As you age, your median life span actually increases, so that once you reach retirement, your median life span is longer.

Let me elaborate. The correct way to think about median life is to imagine a group (or, in the language of statisticians, a cohort) of 100,000 Canadian baby boys (girls), all born, for the sake of argument, in 1996. And let's assume that we were tracking this large group of males and females as they progressed through the human life cycle. Unfortunately, as we know, a small percentage will not survive infancy. Others will succumb to illness or accident in their teenage years, while many more will die in their twenties, thirties, and forties.

Indeed, with the help of actuaries and demographers, Statistics Canada estimates that in 78.6 years (84.3 for females), only 50,000 individuals will be left from the original group of 100,000. Half the group will have died prior to age 78.6 (84.3). In other words, males and females at birth have a 50% chance of reaching age 78.6 and 84.3 respectively.

However, and here's the clincher, if you are still alive at age 65, you have a much greater than 50/50 chance of living out the full statistical term. That's because at 65, you have already survived many potentially fatal illnesses, maladies, and accidents.

The numbers confirm this. In fact, if we were to perform the experiment slightly differently and track a cohort of 100,000 males (females) who were 70 years old in 1996, many more than 50,000 would still be alive by age 78.6 (84.3). Indeed, for this particular cohort of 70-year-olds, half would survive to the ripe old age of 83 (87). We can therefore state that the median life span for a 70-year-old male (female) is 83 (87), which is roughly four or five years more than the equivalent numbers at birth.

As the table below indicates, this process continues at ages 75, 80, 85, and so on.

Table 9.1

Median Life Span at Current Age

Current Age	Female	Male
55	86.3	81.2
65	86.6	81.9
70	87.1	82.9
75	87.9	84.5
85	91.8	90.1
95	98.1	97.4

(Source: See Appendix)

It's also interesting to note that, as you age, the gap between males and females decreases. By age 95, both males and females have between two and three years left to live on average. Moreover, the rate at which life expectancy increases accelerates at age 65. Prior to that age, the numbers are relatively flat, with most deaths occurring in the early years of life.

An analogy that I find helpful is to imagine an unbiased roulette wheel in a casino. The odds of the ball landing on red or black in any particular spin of the wheel is exactly 50/50. If you spin the wheel six times, the odds of landing on red six times in a row are $(0.5)^6$, which is about 1.5% — very small, I would say. In other words, it's a pretty safe bet that you will not see a six-red episode.

But if you spun the wheel five times, and they all came up red, the odds of the next (the sixth) spin being red *are still 50%*. This is a manifestation of what is known as "event conditioning." Once you have more information, the odds change. Conditional on hitting five reds in a row, the odds of hitting another red are still 50%.

The following table should give you a sense of what the actual probabilities are like, in the context of human mortality. I have chosen age 65 as the standard baseline for retirement, although similar numbers can be generated for any age.

Table 9.2

What Are the Chances of Living to Various Ages?

(Current age is 65)

Live-to Age	Female	Male
70	94.0%	89.2%
75	85.5%	75.1%
80	73.4%	57.6%
85	56.6%	38.2%
90	35.9%	20.1%
95	18.6%	7.5%

(Source: Statistics Canada 1996; see Appendix)

As you can see, a male aged 65 stands a 38.2% chance — greater than one in three — of actually reaching age 85. That means, of course, that he'd be spending 20 years of his life in retirement. A 65-year-old female stands a 56.6% chance — greater than one in two — of reaching age 85. In fact, there's an astonishing 35.9% chance (better than one in three) that a 65-year-old female will live until age 90 and spend 25 years in retirement.

This means, once again, that from today's cohort of 100,000 65-year-old females, 35,900 are likely to still be around in 25 more years. In the same manner, 18.6%, or 18,600, are likely to be alive in 30 years.

One final, interesting exercise is to take a male and female couple, both aged 65, and estimate the chances that at least one will still be alive at age 90. This will give you a sense of how to budget for couples as opposed to individuals.

Here's how the calculation is performed. There are, of course, four possibilities: Event #1 — both are dead by age 90; Event #2 — both are alive at age 90; Event #3 — the husband is alive and the wife is dead at age 90; and Event #4 — the wife is alive and the husband is dead at age 90. Mathematically, the probabilities of these four events must add up to 100%. In other words, (Probability of Event #1) + (Probability of Event #2) + (Probability of Event #3) + (Probability of Event #4) = 100%.

To calculate the chances that at least one of them will live to 90, then, we simply have to subtract from 100% the probability that *both* will die by age 90 (Event #1). Then we will be left with the sum of the probabilities of the three events we are interested in: both husband and wife are alive (#2); the husband is alive and the wife is dead (#3); and, the wife is alive and the husband is dead (#4).

This means that 100% – (PE#1) = (PE#2) + (PE#3) + (PE#4). The odds that neither of them survive (PE#1) are calculated by multiplying the odds of the wife not surviving to 90 (which we can figure from Table 9.2 to be 1 – 0.359) by the odds of the husband not surviving (1 – 0.201). The result is (1 – 0.359) x (1 – 0.201) = 0.512, which is a 51.2% chance. So when we subtract the probabilities of neither surviving from 100%, we get 100% – 51.2% = 48.8%. Therefore, 48.8% is the probability that at least one will survive to age 90. Contrast that with the wife's and husband's individual chances of living to age 90 (35.9% and 20.1%, respectively); the idea is that with high certainty, at least one will get to that age.

Interestingly enough, the numbers in Table 9.2 represent an average across all socioeconomic levels of Canadian society. As such, they are probably a downward-biased estimate of how long you will live. As many studies have shown, wealth and health are correlated. By the mere fact that you are reading this book, you are probably wealthier and healthier than average. This is known in the insurance industry as "adverse selection" — meaning that people who buy life annuities tend to live longer than average. As we shall see, insurance companies are well aware of this phenomenon and often adjust their annuity prices to reverse the implications of the self-selection process.

Now that we have seen how long people are living in retirement, let's look at how the insurance companies use that information to price annuities.

How Does an Annuity Work?

In its most general form, purchasing a life annuity (whether joint, fixed-term, or single) involves paying a non-refundable lump sum to an insurance company in exchange for a guaranteed, constant monthly or quarterly income.

With some products, the income ends after a pre-determined or fixed period of time; these are called fixed-term annuities. With other products, the income ends with death. These are known as life annuities. Obviously, a person cannot outlive the income from a life annuity; this is one of the product's strong selling points. No matter how long you live, how markets perform, or what happens to interest rates or the economy as a whole, you will always get a monthly cheque. (The Canadian Life and Health Insurance Compensation Corporation, introduced in 1990, will provide coverage for up to $2,000 per month, in the event of an insolvency on the part of the insurer.)

Annuities, in other words, are a type of longevity insurance — the exact opposite of traditional life insurance. We buy annuities because we are afraid of living too long and will need income to support those extra years of life. We buy life insurance because we are afraid of dying too soon and leaving family and loved ones in financial need.

Insurance companies can provide this lifelong benefit by (a) pooling a large enough group of annuitants and (b) making a very careful and conservative assumption about the rate of return earned on its assets. The pooling of annuitants means that individuals who do not reach their life expectancy, as calculated by actuarial mortality tables, will end up subsidizing those who exceed it.

Table 9.3

Sample Annuity Quotes

($100,000 buys monthly payments for life)

Current Age	Female	Male
55	$533	$591
65	$630	$730
70	$712	$844
75	$832	$1,008
80	$1,014	$1,250

(Source: Annuity broker; see Appendix)

As Table 9.3 suggests, in the current interest-rate environment — and these numbers may change on a weekly basis — a 65-year-old single female with $100,000 can purchase an annuity that will provide her with $630 per month for the rest of her life, no matter how long she lives. The same $100,000 will buy an annuity that will provide a male with the greater amount of $730 per month for life. The additional $100 per month, or 16%, that a male will receive is a direct result of his lower life expectancy.

Remember that our cohort of 65-year-old men can expect to live 17 more years; our cohort of 65-year-old females, on the other hand, can expect to live 22 more years, on average. If the money must last for longer, the payments must be smaller. In fact, this is roughly how insurance companies determine how much to pay out on a life annuity. They estimate the number of years they will be paying, and then "solve for" or calculate a monthly payment that will make things balance out.

You can therefore view a life annuity as a bet with the insurance company. You are betting (and hoping) that you will exceed your cohort's median life span; they are betting (and perhaps hoping) that you will not. Of course, they wish you personally no harm, but your prolonged health is definitely not their first priority.

With that in mind, if the 65-year-old exceeds the median life span of approximately 17 (22) more years, he (she) will have won the bet, and will end up earning a return that is greater than the average interest rate that applied at the time of purchase. If he or she falls short of the median life span, the return will be inferior.

One further important fact to note is that insurance actuaries use mortality tables that are biased toward a long life. They do not really use Statistics Canada tables to calculate life expectancy and mortality probabilities; they use tables that assume people live longer than the population average.

Why?

This, again, is known as adverse selection or, more affectionately, the "lemon problem." The reason that used cars sell for much less than newer ones is because buyers are suspicious of the motives of sellers and demand a lower price to compensate for the uncertainty. (In other words, is the car being sold because it's a lemon?)

In a similar fashion, insurance companies are wary of people who are willing to bet that they will live longer than the average. (Do the buyers of annuities know something that the insurance company doesn't? Is grandma still alive at 102?) To mitigate the mortality risk, they therefore price the life annuity with the healthiest people in mind.

Perhaps, stretching the imagination, we might compare purchasing a life annuity to an all-you-can-eat buffet at your favourite restaurant. Initially, it always seems like a good deal because you can eat as much as you want. "What a bargain," you think to yourself. "I can eat as much as I want at a fixed price."

But think again. The restaurant owners know what they are doing. The buffet is priced to take into account the eating habits and capacity of the average diner. Furthermore, the restaurant will factor in the principle of adverse selection. Chances are, if you choose the buffet, you are hungrier than average — thinking that you will get a better deal because you will be eating so much. The only way you "win the bet" on the buffet is if you eat more than the average consumer. But remember: we are not just talking about *any average* consumer; we are talking about the average consumer *who actually chooses the buffet.*

Another interesting aspect of life annuities is that the monthly payments that you can receive increase the longer you wait before buying the annuity. As noted, for example, a 65-year-old male (female) can get $730 ($630) per month from a $100,000 annuity. But if they waited another 10 years to make the purchase, until age 75, the male (female) would get $1,008 ($832), for life. That's an increase of approximately 35%, simply for deferring the purchase for 10 years.

What's the catch? Once again, median life span is the key. At age 75, a man's median life span is 84.5 years (87.9 for women). This translates into an average of 10 (13) more years of payments, as opposed to 17 (22) more years when you annuitize at age 65. The fewer years the age cohort is likely to live, the larger monthly payments will be. So the lesson is: the longer you wait, the more you will get per month.

Of course, we are cheating a bit because we are comparing apples and oranges. If you annuitize at age 65, you start receiving your monthly cheque immediately, whereas if you wait for 10 years, you won't receive any payments during that period. And if you need to withdraw and consume funds from the $100,000, you will then have less than $100,000 left in 10 years' time. I'll come back to this point later on.

Once again, the key thing to remember is that buying an annuity is synonymous with betting that you will live longer than average — or not caring particularly if you don't. (Don't choose the buffet unless you are very hungry.)

Alternatives to a Life Annuity

The natural alternative to buying a life annuity is the do-it-yourself annuity. In the life insurance lexicon, consumers are familiar with the concept of "buy term and invest the difference." The premise of this approach is that investors can earn a better rate of return than the insurer will pay and should therefore only purchase the pure insurance component.

As you probably know, there are two basic categories of life insurance. The first one is called whole-life (also known as permanent) insurance and the second major category is known as term insurance. Whole-life consists of a savings component and an insurance component. Term, on the other hand, simply consists of an insurance component — and obviously costs less in annual premiums. The reason people tend to buy whole-life is because they would like to save money for the future. Insurance companies bundle the savings and insurance components into one annual premium. It's like buying a fax and printer in one. Maybe it saves space. Maybe it saves money.

The point is, in this context, that individuals are usually counselled to buy term insurance and manage their own savings themselves.

Similarly, you can manage — or create — your own annuity. For example, the retiring 65-year-old male (female) can keep the $100,000 invested in the RRSP for the next few years and then convert the RRSP to a RRIF, while at the same time withdrawing a fixed monthly income of exactly $730 ($630). That, you will remember, is the hypothetical annuity amount that the insurance company would have provided at age 65. (As far as taxes are concerned, the entire $730 will be subject to ordinary income tax rates, regardless of whether the funds are in an RRSP/RRIF or from a life annuity.)

But what if you live too long? Will your money last? Indeed, this do-it-yourself strategy runs a serious financial risk: underfunding retirement in the event of long-run inferior investment returns in conjunction with unexpected human longevity.

Here's my compromise solution and recommended strategy: a modification I call the "do-it-yourself-and-then-switch-if-you-want" strategy. It offers some great odds. Here's how it works. The RRSP is initially converted to a RRIF and depleted at the same rate as a hypothetical life annuity would have provided. Then, after a number of years, the retiree collapses the RRIF and purchases a life annuity.

My thinking runs as follows. At the retirement age of 65, a male (female) can easily beat the mortality-adjusted rate of return from a life annuity for at least 10 or 15 more years. You can do this by investing the funds in an RRSP/RRIF, assuming that you withdraw exactly the same amount that a hypothetical annuity would have provided. Then, in about 10 or 15 years, you have a very good chance of being able to acquire precisely the same $730 ($630)-per-month life annuity, using your remaining wealth.

So what exactly are the odds of success here? What are the chances that you can purchase precisely the same $730 ($630)-per-month life annuity in the future by following this do-it-yourself-and-then-switch strategy?

Here are some numbers. I'll explain in a minute how I arrived at them.

Table 9.4

Probability of Successful Deferral

(Individual age is 65)

Deferral Period	Female	Male
5 years	91%	87%
10 years	93%	89%
15 years	94%	90%

(Source: Author's estimates; see Appendix)

Before I get into the details, let me reiterate that by "probability of successful deferral," I mean the probability that the following strategy will work.

1. A 65-year-old male (female) keeps the $100,000 in his or her RRSP and invests the money in a diversified RRSP/RRIF portfolio, instead of buying a life annuity from an insurance company.
2. At the same time, the male (female) sets up a systematic plan to withdraw $730 ($630) per month, for the next five, 10, or 15 years. This $730 ($630) per month, remember, is not arbitrary. Rather, it is the hypothetical amount that a life annuity would have provided at age 65.
3. In five, 10, or 15 years, the remaining funds in the portfolio — the exact amount of which will depend on how your investments have performed during that period — are used to purchase a life annuity from an insurance company.
4. If the monthly annuity that results is greater than $730 ($630), we can say that the deferral was successful. If the monthly annuity that results is less than $730 ($630), then we would have to conclude that the deferral was a failure.

As Table 9.4 shows, a 65-year-old male (female) has an 87% (91%) chance of being able to purchase the exact same annuity five years from now. He (she) has an 89% (93%) chance of being able to purchase the exact same life annuity 10 years from now.

The odds for the male, you will note, are slightly lower than for the female. Why? Simply because the do-it-yourself part involves a higher level of consumption, which naturally leaves less funds for investment.

You might be asking yourself — just about now — "Where in the world did he get those numbers? How does he know that those are the odds? How does he know if I'll have enough to buy the life annuity in 5, 10, or 15 years?"

These are all very good questions. Let me try to explain.

As you may recall, one of the main themes in this book is that your financial future is random, uncertain, and unpredictable. So any financial projections that ignore the uncertainty — or that don't tell you the odds — are giving you half the picture at best. However, although it is impossible to predict, you *can* ask questions, and get meaningful answers, about your financial future by using Monte Carlo computer simulations. The computer simulations can give you the probability of regret from choosing various courses of action. These are the same kind of simulations I described in Chapter 8. In that chapter I was focusing on the question of a suitable mix between stocks and bonds; this time I am looking at the annuity question. Specifically, to get the probability of regret on the deferral strategy, I simulated millions of individuals — at various ages — who all withdraw the fixed amount the annuity would have provided each and every month. After running these scenarios, and looking at how much money people had left after five, 10, 15, and 20 years, I counted the number of scenarios in which they had enough to buy the exact same life annuity they originally contemplated. Sometimes they didn't have enough left, but — overwhelmingly — most times they did.

This Monte Carlo computer simulation was somewhat

trickier than in the retirement asset allocation case, mainly because I had to keep track of two different things. First of all, I had to monitor each individual's wealth over the next 20 years. But I also had to keep track of exactly how much the insurance companies were likely to charge for life annuities during the next 20 years. This more complicated exercise involved making assumptions about mortality patterns, insurance loads, and interest rates. You can read the end-of-chapter notes in the Appendix if this interests you further.

Nevertheless — and taking into account the complex nature of this computer simulation — let me try to give you some financial intuition for *why* the odds of a successful deferral are so high. Specifically, why is it that you most probably will have enough money left over in five, 10, or even 15 years to buy exactly the same life annuity you could buy today?

I think it's important to get a sense for the *why*, even though the precise numbers seen in Table 9.4 can only be obtained using the computer simulations I described.

I'll try to approach this in a couple of different ways, but please bear in mind that in my explanation I'm going to assume that interest rates will remain constant at 5%, just to make things easier to understand. Certainly, in real life, the whole point of my analysis was to examine the what-if scenarios where things do not stay the same. Keeping this in mind, here is one way to think about this whole deferral business.

Let's revisit Table 9.3, with its sample annuity quotes, and use the numbers in a slightly different way. If a 65-year-old female gets a monthly $630 per $100,000, then she is paying roughly $100,000 divided by (12 x $630) = $13.23 for each $1 of lifetime yearly income.

Similarly, if a 75-year-old female earns a monthly $832 per $100,000, then she is paying about $100,000 divided by (12 x $832) = roughly $10.02 for each $1 of lifetime yearly income. As you can quickly see, this yearly income — with a lifetime guarantee — becomes $3.21 "cheaper" if the 65-year-old female waits 10 more years before buying the annuity.

Why is it cheaper? Because the 75-year-old has less time left in the human life cycle compared to the 65-year-old. The same amount of money, $100,000, returned with interest over a shorter period of time, translates into more money per month.

But, in fact, it's not just cheaper by $3.21, because we are comparing prices across 10 different years. Because of inflation and the time-value of money, that $10.02 10 years from now would be worth a lot less than $10.02 today. So to get a better sense of how much "cheaper" the annuity will be if you waited 10 years, you must subtract the *present value* of $10.02 ($6.15 when the interest rate is 5%) from the current price of $13.23. Stated differently, if you invested $6.15 for 10 years at 5% per annum, you would have exactly $10.02 in 10 years. So the true measure of how much cheaper the annuity would become by waiting 10 years is $13.23 – $6.15 = $7.08.

But the $7.08 is for *each dollar* of income per year. Now let's convert back to the original numbers. You'll recall that the $630 per month that a female can obtain from a life annuity purchased at age 65 translates into 12 x $630 = $7,560 per year. Therefore, by waiting 10 years, she would "save" $7.08 x $7,560 = $53,525 from her initial wealth of $100,000.

I use the word "save" in conjunction with the sum of $53,525 because it represents the amount from the $100,000 that you *don't need* in order to buy the annuity in 10 years. You only need the remaining $46,475.

Of course, we must be careful here not to abuse the word "save." If you annuitize today, at age 65, you earn monthly payments of $630 for life, starting immediately. On the

MONEY LOGIC

other hand, if you annuitize in 10 years, at age 75, you don't receive the $630 monthly payments during the next decade. So you're not really *saving* $53,525, because you'll surely need to draw on some of those funds in order to live, until the annuity is purchased. There is, in other words, no free lunch.

Still, if you can invest the $53,525 and successfully withdraw $630 per month for the next 10 years, then it is worthwhile to wait before you annuitize. This is not a personal decision about whether you can live on $630 per month; rather, it's a matter of whether you can invest your money and earn a higher return than the insurance company is implicitly giving you during the next 10 years.

So when I speak of "successful" withdrawal, I mean that you are able to earn a high enough rate of return on your $53,525 so that, consuming that $630 per month, you do not exhaust your funds before the end of the 10-year period. Remember, you are actually investing the entire $100,000. But the remaining $46,475 (invested in relatively safe assets) has been mentally set aside for the annuity purchase in 10 years' time. In sum, you are living on $53,525 for the next 10 years.

Obviously, financial success and failure has a probability attached to it. Indeed, that is exactly what I am trying to compute. I'm examining the odds that you can bake your own annuity — consuming the same $630 every month — and still have enough left over to buy the annuity, if you so desire, later on in the life cycle.

As Figure 9.1 illustrates, I am advocating that you mentally split your initial capital of $100,000 into two parts. The first part, $53,525, you will invest and live on for the next 10 years. The second part, the remaining $46,475, you will ideally place in an investment that is negatively correlated with interest rates — so that you can purchase your annuity in 10 years' time.

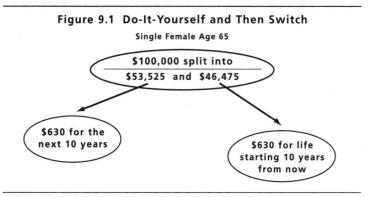

Figure 9.1 Do-It-Yourself and Then Switch

Single Female Age 65

$100,000 split into
$53,525 and $46,475

$630 for the
next 10 years

$630 for life
starting 10 years
from now

In practice, the negative correlation simply means that you put the $46,475 in an investment that is more likely to appreciate the lower interest rates get (even though in this simple example, I assumed that rates are constant at 5%). A balanced portfolio of common equities and long-term bonds provides a good example of investments that would increase in value if interest rates fall. In this manner, if annuity payouts decrease during the next 10 years, your portfolio will increase in value, and you'll be able to afford exactly the same annuity stream.

Of course, this is where the probability argument comes in — and why I had to conduct the Monte Carlo computer simulation. What are the odds that you can withdraw $630 per month — for the next 10 years — from your $53,525? Similarly, what are the odds that the remaining $46,475 can be invested so that you can buy exactly the same annuity in 10 years? Indeed, the numbers in Table 9.4 seem to indicate high odds.

I promised two ways to intuitively understand the computer results. Here is an additional explanation for why it is so much more appealing and logical to annuitize at age 75 or 80 rather than at age 65. Table 9.5 is a supplement to Table 9.3. It shows the internal rate of return (IRR) — a measure of profitability — from purchasing a life annuity

with $100,000 at various ages, assuming that you will live
and receive payments until age 95.

Table 9.5

You purchase a life annuity with $100,000.

What is your IRR, assuming you live to age 95?

Purchase Age	Female	Male
65	6.66%	8.24%
75	8.22%	11.17%
80	9.37%	13.54%
85	10.00%	19.62%

(Source: Annuity Values from Table 9.3)

Table 9.5 states that if an 80-year-old male purchases a
life annuity, and survives to age 95 — thus receiving $1,250
per month for 15 years — he will earn an implicit 13.54%
annual return on his initial investment. It is implicit because
when you discount 15 years of $1,250 monthly payments, at
a rate of 13.54% per year, you obtain the original $100,000.
(Think of it like a $100,000 home mortgage amortized at
13.54% over a 15-year period, with monthly payments of
$1,250.)

The same purchase at age 85 provides an even better
yield — an implicit 19.62% annual return. A 19.62% return is
very high and would clearly be difficult to beat using alternative investment classes. However, at age 65, the internal
rate of return is much lower (8.24%), even with the assumption that you live to age 95.

This 8.24%, then, becomes your threshold. If you can
earn that return, or greater, using alternative investment
vehicles, then it's worthwhile to wait. If you can't beat the
8.24% — with reasonable probability — then you should
buy the annuity. Therefore, another reason for deferring
the decision to annuitize — retaining the option to *eventually* annuitize — is that the implicit rate of return is quite

low to begin with, at age 65, but becomes virtually impossible to beat, at later ages, using alternative investment classes.

Of course, once again, some caveats are in order. First, there is no guarantee that annuity prices for a 75-year-old will remain — in the example of the 75-year-old female — at $832 per $100,000, or in other words at $10.02 per $1 of lifetime income. In fact, the $832 could decrease (and thus the $10.02 may increase), if interest rates were to decline over the next 10 years. That's why I am more likely to advocate this deferral strategy in a low-interest-rate environment, where the probability of further reductions over the next 10 years is small.

Second, to the detriment of the buyer, even without a decline in interest rates, insurance companies may decide to change their mortality assumptions to incorporate longer life spans, thus reducing the monthly payment. However, to counteract this argument, I claim that the probability of illness, and the value of keeping your options open, outweighs this particular risk.

It is very important to stress that this strategy only works if the RRSP/RRIF — in other words, the funds you will later use to buy the deferred annuity — are invested in a well-diversified way. Putting the funds in a low-interest-bearing Guaranteed Investment Certificate defeats the point, and would likely make it impossible to ever purchase the same annuity in the future. In our previous example, the $7.08 must be invested using a high allocation to equity in order to generate the $1 per year, for 10 years.

Of course, the flip side to this argument is the incredible value that one gets from annuitizing at older ages, when the individual may not be concerned with leaving an estate. Take the 80-year-old male in Table 9.3, for example. He earns $1,250 per month for every $100,000. This implies a cost of $100,000 divided by (12 x $1,250) = $6.67 for every

$1 of yearly lifetime income. It is difficult to generate that kind of return from conventional instruments.

Of course, an obvious question to ask about this approach is, why bother? What's the purpose of not buying a life annuity now if you're going to buy it in 10 years and withdraw the same amount each month anyway? Why bother with an elaborate strategy that may not even work?

The answer to this question is twofold. First, you as the retiree maintain complete control over your funds, which means that your liquidity is maintained. Thus, any emergency or unforeseen cash crunch, especially for long-term care, can be met from the non-annuitized pool. Second, you retain the *option* to annuitize at any time. Why pay for something today if, in all probability, you can pay for it in 10 years with no real increase in cost, and no diminishment in the benefits of the purchase?

An additional factor is inflation. Most of today's annuities are largely inadequate in protecting against inflation. (There are annuities available that protect you from inflation — so-called "real annuities" — but they are relatively more expensive.) Maintaining control of the funds allows you to hedge the inflation risk by purchasing assets that tend to increase in inflationary periods. Annuitization is akin to purchasing a Government of Canada bond with amortized principal and souped-up coupons. The coupons are higher than normal because the bond is completely non-transferable and goes with you to the grave. As many of us have learned the hard way, unexpected inflation — together with a general increase in interest rates — will wreak havoc on bond prices. The same thing goes for annuities.

Even though they are not traded in the marketplace, annuities still lose theoretical value when interest rates increase. Those who think that inflation is permanently dead should ask themselves why the spread between yields on real and nominal bonds in Canada (summer of 1998) is at 1%–2%. In other words, very roughly speaking, investors are expecting at least 1%–2% inflation per year, over the next 30 years. This means that, at 2%, your $730 ($630) per month will only be worth half as much, in today's dollars, 30 years from now. And if our 65-year-old couple doesn't worry that far ahead, then he (and she) shouldn't be purchasing a life annuity in the first place.

The Bequest Motive

There is one additional reason for deferring (and perhaps even avoiding, in some cases) the decision to annuitize as long as prudently possible — the bequest motive. Purchasing a pure life annuity will leave nothing for the estate. Remember that with a straight life annuity, payments cease with your death. The worst-case scenario, which many people fear, is that you hand over $100,000 to the insurance company, which promises you monthly cheques for the rest of your life; then, a few months later, you die. The monthly cheques stop coming, the remaining portion of the $100,000 rightfully belongs to the insurance company, and your estate is left with nothing. If there *is* a guarantee period, which of course you pay for, the monthly payments will continue until the guarantee period is over. So in that sense, the estate, children, or loved ones will get something.

Nevertheless, the whole idea of annuity purchases involves the pooling of risk. The living are subsidized by the dying. In fact, in some provinces, annuitants must receive written permission from their spouses — kept on file by the insurance company — in order to buy a single life annuity.

With this in mind, the longer you can defer annuitization, the greater the chances — morbid though this may sound — that you will die prior to purchasing the life annuity. That means your estate inherits the proceeds of the RRIF. Taxes will complicate things, but marginal tax rates are still far less than 100%, so there will always be something left over.

CONCLUSION

Contemporary economics has developed a technique known as option pricing theory. One of the things it teaches us is that having the right — but not the obligation — to buy something is valuable and should be exercised, with appropriate caution. A decision that is irreversible (like buying a life annuity) should only be undertaken when the potential value of keeping the option alive is worth less than the immediate benefit of exercising the option. That, for example, is why exchange-traded stock options are rarely exercised early.

The same concept applies to the irreversible purchase of a life annuity. RRIFs can always be converted to annuities, but annuities can never be converted to RRIFs. For individuals who are willing to tolerate a minimal probability of shortfall, it therefore makes very little sense in my judgment to convert an RRSP to a life annuity at age 69. The odds say that it makes more sense to wait.

What Is a Risky Future?

I want to conclude with a question: What do you consider financial risk to be? Is financial risk synonymous with price volatility, market fluctuations, terrifying headlines, and day-to-day uncertainty? One week the Toronto Stock Exchange average gains 5%; the next week, it loses 10%. One quarter, your mutual fund earns 27%; wonderful. But the next quarter, it loses 34%; not so wonderful. Is this financial risk to you? If it is, then national and international stock markets — especially given the volatility of 1998 — are definitely a place to avoid.

And you wouldn't be alone. For bureaucrats, corporate executives, central bankers, elected politicians, and even mutual fund managers market turmoil is also a very risky business. In many cases, their lucrative jobs may be at stake.

These people have to be seen trying to do something. Often, they are damned if they do and damned if they don't.

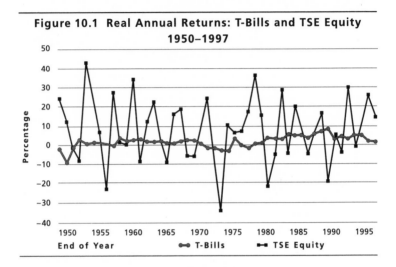

Figure 10.1 Real Annual Returns: T-Bills and TSE Equity 1950–1997

Take a look at Figure 10.1. It seems to conform to the volatility view of financial risk. It shows — side by side — the year-over-year (after-inflation) returns from the Canadian stock market and Canadian treasury bills. For every year since 1950, it indicates how much you would have earned from investing your money in treasury bills and how much you would have earned from a diversified portfolio in the Canadian stock market.

So you tell me, which asset class is risky and which asset class is safe? If market fluctuations are your preferred measure of risk, then the answer is a no-brainer. Equity markets will take you on a wild and volatile ride. They are, in that sense, *risky*. Short-term debt instruments, on the other hand, are *safe*. Safe means stable. It means year-to-year predictability. It means no surprises.

However — and here is the essence of my thesis — for individuals facing personal financial decisions (namely, all of us), I'm not convinced that volatility and fluctuations capture the true measure of financial risk. To me, financial risk is something much more intuitive and definitive than some jagged lines generated on a well-designed graph.

Financial decision making, as we saw in the Introduction, has much to learn from the science of weather forecasting. Issues of financial risk, I submit, should be framed and explained in terms of what I have called the Probability of Regret (PoR). Financial risk is the probability that you will look back — with 20/20 hindsight — and regret the original decision. Financial risk is measured by the probability that you could or would have done better by simply going with the safe, risk-free solution.

If you are willing to accept shortfall and regret as the relevant risk in your life — and this may not be easy — then financial risk has an embedded dimension of time. It is meaningless to talk about risk without talking about an appropriate time horizon over which you are contemplating the investment decision.

Is the stock market risky? Well, that depends. Using only a short-term horizon, it's absolutely risky. Using a long-term horizon, I would argue that most equity markets *probably* are not. Are GICs, treasury bills, Canada Savings Bonds, and term deposits safe? Well, once again, that depends on time. In the short term, they're the safest things available. After all, they are implicitly guaranteed by federal and provincial authorities. Their returns are reliable and predictable. But, in the same manner, I would argue that over the long term, such investments are *risky*.

How can that be? If it's safe to hold a guaranteed Canada Savings Bond for one year, why is it risky to hold it for 10? Once again, it comes down to how you feel about risk. If you consider risk (as I argue) to be the probability of regret (PoR), then I believe that in the long run, you will regret the decision to invest in these instruments because the other asset classes will do better. The odds that equity markets will perform worse than these apparently safe instruments decline exponentially over time. The longer you own the equity asset class, the lower will be your probability of regret. The longer you hold the equity asset class, the lower the odds that you will look back and say: "Oh, what a mistake I made!" Look back at the chart in the Introduction: the shortfall risk of regret declines as the time horizon lengthens.

Of course, I am not counselling recklessness. Caution is warranted here. And I'm certainly not dismissing the importance of short-term GICs, CSBs, term deposits, and money market funds. They are the only vehicles to use — the only place to park your money — if your goals are strictly short term. Perhaps you're planning to buy a house in a few years, and are saving for a downpayment. Perhaps your car has an overdue appointment with the wrecker, and you're saving for a new one. Perhaps you want a new boat or a new cottage or even a new dining room set? These are short-horizon objectives; the money to fund these needs should *only* be placed in short-term, risk-free guaranteed instruments. Those who ignored — or plan to ignore — this advice should think back to the capital-eroding third quarter of 1998. Short-term money has no place in a long-term game.

All your investment adviser, financial planner, or stock-broker can do is give you the odds — the probability of regret. But only you can decide whether to take an umbrella.

So how long should you plan for? What is your time horizon? How long are you likely to live and what are the odds of reaching that age? Chapter 9 gave us a very good indication of the probabilities of reaching various ages. As I argued, the odds of living into your eighties or nineties are today quite favourable. Remember, it's not just the median life span — or the average — that matters. It's the odds of reaching advanced ages.

More important, it's not just your *physical* time horizon
that matters; your *mental* time horizon is even more crucial. In fact, it's your mental horizon that will determine
how much risk you can bear.
Do you have a short- or a long-term mental horizon? How
can you tell? Well, do you wake up at 3:00 a.m. worrying
about how the Japanese markets are doing and how they
will affect the next day's trading on North American markets? Is the mutual fund section of your daily newspaper
the first thing you look at with your morning coffee? Is
your Internet browser set to four different websites that
give you up-to-the-minute values of your investments? Do
you hang up on your spouse when your broker calls?

If your answer to any of the above is yes, then I would
venture to guess that you certainly don't have a long-term
investment horizon. You may *claim* to be investing for the
long run, but that's just lip service. Your daily actions contradict that dispassionate, I'm-here-for-the-duration philosophy.
You are basically acting like a myopic short-term investor.

What's the difference between long and short term?
What happens in the long term that is so different from the
year-over-year behaviour? Compare Figure 10.1 with Figure

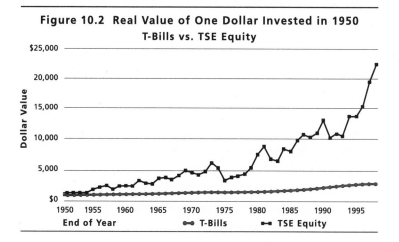

**Figure 10.2 Real Value of One Dollar Invested in 1950
T-Bills vs. TSE Equity**

203

10.2. In Figure 10.2, you see what the cumulative (after-inflation) results would be of investing one dollar in the equity markets and one dollar in the treasury bill markets, from 1950 until September 1998. Look at the gap. Look at the margin. Where is the place to be — after all is said and done — and which investment would you regret?

Figure 10.1 seems to contradict Figure 10.2. In Figure 10.1, equities seem historically the riskier asset class, their behaviour volatile, unpredictable, and uncertain. Yet in Figure 10.2, equities completely beat treasury bills. So are equity markets safe, or are they risky? Well, here we go again. It all comes down to time horizon. In the long term, the risk declines. In the long term, the risk is mitigated. Why is that so? Why should equity markets go up in the long term? Why should they beat the performance of other asset classes? Why should they give you the best odds? What's the catch? Why should I be rewarded — *just for waiting*? How do we know that the past is any indication of the future? True, for the last 50 years, the risk of equity investments declined over time. But who says the next 50 years will mirror that pattern?

It all comes down to risk and reward. If you're willing to live with short-term risk — willing to tolerate short-term fluctuations and day-to-day volatility — you will be compensated in the long run. If you can't handle the short term, if the uncertainty is stressful and the headlines are unbearable, then the markets are too hot for you: get out of the kitchen. You don't have the right horizon. You don't have the right risk profile. You don't have the right psychological makeup for stock market exposure. At the same time, of course, you will not be entitled to the long-term rewards.

But what if your neighbour or broker gives you a hot, can't-miss stock tip? What if you hear about a wonderful new high-tech company that's just about to go public with its first share offering? What if you read about a great new stock in the newspaper? Inevitably, these kinds of things happen. But I would ask: Is this really the way to choose equity investments?

You may think you're getting in on the ground floor, before the rest of the investment world has discovered your new jewel. In all likelihood, you're wrong. This, I would argue, is a mug's game. It's a waste of money and, more importantly, a loss of future confidence in the stock market, which will hit you when you realize that the stock has fizzled, or has failed to keep pace with the broader market. Remember, you are competing against thousands of highly skilled analysts who spend their days — and much of their nights — poring over financial statements and annual reports looking for the next big hit. Count on it: you will be out-numbered, out-smarted and out-maneuvered by the competition. Stick to your day job.

Yes, your golfing buddy, good old Chuck, bought a stock that tripled in a week. But did he tell you about all the tip-based investments he made that went nowhere? This is survivorship bias. You only hear about the winners. So it doesn't matter if this company is on the verge of inventing a perpetual motion machine that will change the world. Just ask yourself this question: "What edge do I have? What gives me better odds than anybody else playing this game?" If you can identify the edge — and it's legal — then go ahead, by all means; take the plunge. Otherwise, stick to investing, not speculating. Remember, if it sounds too good to be true, you haven't been listening carefully.

Think of such investment opportunities as you would if you were reading that wonderful children's book series *Where's Waldo?* He's hiding there somewhere; that we know. The challenge is to find him, cleverly camouflaged among the crowd. Similarly, I enjoy looking for the hidden risk in the can't-lose propositions.

Although I hate rules of thumb — especially when it

comes to money and finance — here is one I feel pretty comfortable with. If somebody *promises* you more than a 30% return on your stock, mutual fund, or limited partnership investment in one year — without any risk to your principal — hang up the phone and call the provincial securities commission.

And let me add this: By singling out 30% as ridiculous, I'm not saying that 25% is a reasonable expectation of profit. All I'm saying is that at the 30% level, you must be taking some very *serious* risks. Most likely, there is leverage lurking there somewhere and, as you will recall from Chapter 7, the downside of leverage can be ugly.

So let's say I've convinced you. What next? Do you call your broker and ask him or her to buy you a couple of good stocks? Pick a few solid companies with decent dividend yields and sturdy business prospects? Or should you go to mutual funds? And if mutual funds are the preferred route, how should you pick one from the scores available?

These questions lead us to the importance of diversification, both national and international (Chapter 4). It's not the number of investments that count; it's how (or whether) they move together that matters. Buying 10 stocks or 10 mutual funds can be just as risky as buying one stock or one fund, if they are all in the same general economic and financial sector. Remember, it's the correlation that counts. Yes, they all should go up over time, but when one investment zigs, you want the other investment to zag. You want to own enough stocks, bonds, etc. to reduce, as much as possible, the probability that you will regret that investment.

In fact, the concept of correlation goes far beyond your simple investment portfolio. It's not just investments in financial capital that should be constructed with low correlation. Investments in your own human capital should also have low correlation with your other investments.

For example, if you work for a high-tech company developing the next must-have computer gadget, website, or software program, don't put all your financial assets in the same high-tech sector as well. Why? These two investments — your human capital and your financial capital — would be highly correlated if they were invested in the same economic sector. In this case, your shortfall risk — the odds of regret — would be very high because, in all likelihood, if your human capital investment suffered, your financial capital would suffer as well.

In fact, there's a strong economic argument to be made for investing part of your financial capital in your biggest competitor's stock. It, I would argue, will be negatively correlated with your human capital. If your company suffers, perhaps your competitor will succeed. In any event, you will have diversified. Yes, you may reduce some upside potential, but you will have definitely reduced your downside risk or probability of regret.

The same concept applies to those working in the financial sector, natural resources, or real estate. Diversify your investment capital so that it is not highly correlated with your human capital. If you are forced to hold a large portion of your wealth in your own company's stock — to align your incentives with those of your shareholders — then make sure you have some sort of downside protection.

But are mutual funds the way to go? Or should you pick these stocks yourself? Well, here is where we probed the question of risk-adjusted performance (Chapter 1). It's not enough to find a fund that makes money, or even to find one fund that did better than average. You have to assess the risk that fund was taking, and whether its performance compensated you appropriately for those risks.

To gain real confidence in the fund, its manager or the company, you must convince yourself that this fund's performance cannot be attributed to chance alone. You must ask yourself: what are the odds that they were just lucky? Sure, there is no guarantee that, if skill was involved, they can continue to deliver positive performances. But if they were merely lucky, there is virtually no hope of persistence. If they have some skill, then at least you have a running chance. Be very selective and cautious. Few fund managers will admit that 60% to 70% of their colleagues do not beat the appropriate indices in the long run. Even fewer will tell you that you can invest in these same averages with no loads and fewer expenses, in the form of index funds, index baskets, and index-linked GICs (Chapter 5).

Of course, there is always concern that one day, week, or month after you put your life savings into the mutual fund of your choice, the stock market will drop 20%. Isn't this the secret nightmare of every investor? So why not invest it slowly, using the technique known as dollar-cost averaging? In that way, you reason, you can avoid the horrendous consequences of picking the wrong time. Well, your intentions are admirable, but the implementation is faulty. As I argued in Chapter 2, dollar-cost averaging will not give you better odds. Lump-sum investing is superior, for the reasons described. This doesn't mean you shouldn't save regularly — that's a great idea. All I'm saying is that dollar-cost averaging will not reduce your volatility more than a simple asset allocation mix between equity and fixed-income securities.

But if lump-sum investing is the right way to go, if the motto is "invest now, when you have the money," then perhaps you should succumb to the temptation to borrow, in order to invest. Many people have done just that, remortgaging their homes and investing the proceeds in the (seemingly) never-faltering stock market.

Needless to say, no matter how you define risk, this strategy is risky. It only makes sense under very limited conditions, as I discussed in Chapter 7. Moreover, you have to distinguish between tax-deductible and non-tax-deductible debt, and make sure that you can afford the interest payments, without having to sell out at the worst possible time. Remember, the odds of losing money are magnified — in the early years — when you borrow.

But if equities are the place to be in the long run, does that mean there is absolutely no chance of regret — or at least of losing money — if I buy a diversified mutual fund and just hold it? Absolutely not!

The risk of shortfall and regret is always present; it may decline with the time horizon, but it will always be there. In fact, this is one of the main reasons that segregated funds (Chapter 3) offering 10-year money-back guarantees are so popular. The odds of regret are slim, but you still have to pay for the insurance, just as you would for your car, home, or even health insurance. The odds are low, but you still pay. Depending on your attitude toward risk, and your ability to sleep at night, you may want to consider Seg funds as an alternative to Reg funds. Remember, the older you are, the more valuable that guarantee will be, especially in light of estate-planning issues.

But at what age is it time to leave the party? After all, are your retirement years really a good time to be playing the stock market and taking (even minimal) shortfall risks? Well, again I would argue that the odds tend to favour a diversified portfolio of equity and fixed-income investments, even in your retirement years, when it's time to collapse the RRSP. With that in mind, I think people should defer the decision to annuitize as long as possible, because the odds are better if you leave your options open. As the computer simulations in Chapter 9 demonstrated, most people were better off waiting. This policy would apply to lump-sum settlements from pensions as well. Any action that you cannot reverse, such as reconverting your pension annuity to a lump sum, should be delayed as long as possible.

In fact, if I were designing my own retirement portfolio at age 65, I would probably invest 100% in the equities market. But immediately after the purchase, I would also buy some put options — funded by selling calls (Chapter 6) — to protect my downside in the event of a sharp correction. As time passed — and if markets moved up enough to completely fund my retirement — I would gradually sell off parts of these puts and calls. Otherwise, I would continue to roll over the options. To make this strategy work better and cost less, I would buy and sell so-called *average rate options*, as opposed to the standard puts and calls. The payoffs of average rate options, unlike *standard options*, are based on the average (as opposed to final) performance of the underlying security over the life of the option. So you end up making money if the average price was above (or under, depending on the type of option) a certain level, not just if the final price on the last day of trading was above (or under) a certain level. In a sense, you are insuring yourself against a long-term growth rate, as opposed to a market price on any particular day. This type of strategy is known as a contingent portfolio insurance scheme, and it is used by many professional institutional investors.

Does it sound too complicated for your personal finances?

Perhaps today, yes. But not 25 years from now. Think about it. Twenty-five years ago, people's personal financial options were pretty simple. After sinking a large portion of your capital into a house, investors could save for the future with stocks and bonds, a standard bank account, and maybe a mutual fund or two. Today, on the other hand, you are faced with a universe of products with exotic-sounding names like collateralized mortgage obligations, index funds, protective puts, segregated mutual funds, real estate income trusts, strips, TIPS, HIPS, index-linked GICs, deferred installment receipts, equity-linked notes, and even inflation-linked bonds. Indeed, I have probably missed a half-dozen other names and investment vehicles. Who knows what the financial products of the future will look like? What financial innovations are we likely to see and what impact will they have on our financial lives? Well, here is a light-hearted view of what the RRSP season in the year 2025 might look like. It's January, the time of year when you think about long-term financial goals and objectives. The annual marketing campaigns from the banks, trust companies, and superstores are about to begin.

Your financial planner and registered nurse are scheduled to arrive in a few minutes to conduct the annual blood test. The test will determine whether there's been any change in your DNA's risk-aversion level.

Years ago, of course, provincial regulators required investors to complete a "know your client form," which guided financial planners in assessing general attitudes toward financial risk. Your risk profile would help them design an appropriate asset allocation, investment portfolio, and mutual fund selection. The legal form also protected them from liability in the unfortunate event that you lost an enormous amount of money — and wanted to sue them for negligence. But widespread fraud on the part of applicants, who constantly lied about their true attitudes toward risk, wreaked havoc on the integrity of the questionnaire process.

Fortunately, in the year 2007, Professors Hi and Lo, two bio-economists at Harvard University, working with a medical team from the National Institutes of Health, were able to isolate the gene that controls financial risk-aversion. Although classical economists had postulated the gene's existence for years, there had been — until its discovery — no empirical evidence that humans were born with a unique and quantifiable attitude toward financial risk. Now, a simple blood test can determine the precise amount of financial risk that an investor is able and willing to tolerate. Inevitably, the Harvard researchers were jointly awarded the Nobel Prize in Economics and Medicine for this groundbreaking discovery.

The Hi & Lo risk-aversion metric is measured on a scale of 0 to 100. Higher numbers are associated with greater abilities to bear risk. Most Hi-Lo zeros exhibit a strong preference for keeping all their money in the form of gold coins buried in a steel case in their backyards; people in the 100 category seem to be completely invested in penny stocks of gold exploration companies in Indonesia.

Gene therapy soon followed, and many option, derivative, and hedge-fund traders were successfully treated to reduce their excessive risk-taking levels.

Federal regulators were quick to jump on the bandwagon, and the "know your client" forms were soon replaced with risk-aversion blood tests, which became affectionately known as "poke your client."

Well, maybe not exactly . . .

Last Words

As a professor, I'm always concerned that, no matter how much I hope for the contrary, my students will remember little — if anything — of my lectures a few months after the term ends. A buzzword here, maybe, or a slogan there, but most of the content will be gone. In a perhaps futile attempt to counteract this inevitable decay of knowledge, I always spend the semester's final lecture hour stressing the main points I want the class to remember — not just during the final exam (their principal priority), but years after I and the course are just blurred memories.

I make a series of statements to the effect of "If you run

into me in a few years, I want you to tell me that you remember the following five things about this course . . ." This valiant effort seems to have had some effect. In fact, on those cheerful occasions when I do run into old students, I am always gratified by their attempts to remind me of that final lecture. But when it comes down to what exactly I had said, the conversation trails off. Oh, well. Perhaps the knowledge is hibernating in their subconscious, waiting to emerge one day, when they really need it, not just to impress me.

So what would I like you to remember, long after this book is collecting dust on your shelf?

Well, I could expound on how important it is to start saving for retirement at a young age. I could tell you that if you stop buying a cup of coffee every morning for the next 30 years — and save that money instead — you'll be able to buy a condo in Florida with the savings, when you retire. I could talk about how much your child's education will cost in 20 years, or how many millions of dollars you'll need to retire in the year 2025. But my bet is that you've already heard these speeches from many other sources.

So I'd rather leave you with a simple, final thought. If there is one thing that's for certain, it's that the future isn't. Your financial future — and its success — depend on a variety of factors, most of which are outside your own and your financial adviser's control. Your financial future is random, uncertain, and unpredictable. What you can do, however, is become knowledgeable about the probabilities of regret associated with various courses of action, and then make decisions that minimize those same probabilities of regret.

I hope this book has given you a good indication of those factors that do — and those that do not — affect the probabilities of regret. If you regard every financial decision, from insurance purchases to monetary investments, as a form of medical surgery, you will constantly ask yourself: "Will this procedure give me the best odds? And if not, why am I doing it?"

Remember, calculate the odds. And then put them to work.

APPENDIX

CHAPTER 1

How Well Did Your Fund Really Do?

This chapter draws on some of the mathematics that Dr. Steven (Eli) Posner (no relation to my colleague on this book) and I developed for our paper entitled: "A theoretical investigation of randomized asset allocation strategies" (Spring 1998 issue of *Applied Mathematical Finance*). However, this topic is somewhat basic to modern investment theory, and was inspired by a paper I read in the Fall 1990 issue of the *Journal of Portfolio Management*, by A. J. Marcus. The author was trying to determine, statistically, whether the performance of Fidelity's Magellan fund could be explained by chance alone. After all, *somebody* has to win the race, and the winner of such a huge contest can be expected to earn phenomenal returns. His conclusion was that Magellan cannot be — surprise, surprise — explained by chance. In fact, distinguishing randomness from skill — and the implicit ranking of risk-adjusted performance — has now become a sophisticated multi-million-dollar consulting industry. However, the basic technique and thinking can be applied to all funds, on the individual level as well. Clearly, the more funds there are in a particular category, the less surprised I am to find one of them beating the index by an eye-popping 2,000 basis points. Also, please note that strictly speaking it is incorrect to interpret the probability of observing a particular data outcome, given the null hypothesis, as a probability that the null hypothesis is correct, given the data. The only way to obtain a posterior probability for the null hypothesis is to assume a probability of the observed event under the alternative, which is equally problematic. Also, from a technical point of view, please note that the numbers reported in Table 1.2 assumed normally distributed returns and excess returns — a strong assumption, given the sample properties. However, the lesson is unfettered: "What are the odds the fund manager was lucky?" is the most important question to ask about any track record.

CHAPTER 2
Dollar-Cost Averaging

This chapter is based on a research paper written with Dr. Steven (Eli) Posner. It examined the continuous time distribution and implications of dollar-cost averaging in relation to its representation as an arithmetic option-pricing problem. The practice of dollar-cost averaging is widespread, and I am skeptical that this chapter will change many minds. Some additional articles that you may find interesting and helpful include: "Lump-sum investing versus dollar-averaging," by M. S. Rozeff in the Winter 1994 issue of the *Journal of Portfolio Management*; "Nobody gains from dollar-cost averaging," by J. R. Knight and L. Mandell, in the 1991/1992 issue of *Financial Services Review*; and "The fallacy of dollar-cost averaging," by S. Thorley in the Fall 1994 issue of the *Journal of Financial Practice and Education*. All of these articles point out the inefficiency of dollar-cost averaging and the more effective alternatives for reducing risk. Of course, I do not question the psychological importance of a systematic savings plan; it's the investment strategy that bothers me, as it does many others.

CHAPTER 3

Segregated Mutual Funds

This chapter is in response to the many (confused) public financial commentators who claim that a 10-year stock market guarantee is worthless, because the Canadian market has never experienced a 10-year decline. That's like saying that your house insurance is not worth anything, because your house has never burned down. Indeed, as I argue, the protection is valuable; it's just a question of whether or not you are overpaying for it. The chapter is based on an actuarial research paper I wrote, entitled: "What is the value of a guarantee?" The Seg fund is basically a Reg fund with a 10-year at-the-money put option attached. As time evolves, the embedded put moves in — but most likely out — of the money. With all (risk-neutral) likelihood, the option will expire out of the money, and above the current strike price. However, the option — at inception — still has value, despite the low probability. Therefore, the underlying idea is to price a 10-year index put option — using the Black-Scholes/Merton model — for various levels of volatility, interest rates, and dividend yields. The price of the option is then amortized over the 10 years and subtracted, as a percentage, from the value of the fund. This becomes the additional MER that should be charged in exchange for the 10-year put. The decision on whether or not to lock in comes down to a decision on whether to swap an out-of-the-money put with a less-than-10-year maturity, in exchange for an at-the-money put with a 10-year maturity. The decision is not trivial, because the time decay factor (known as theta) can be positive. Indeed, more time can be worse. As I mentioned in the chapter, the value of being able to lock in is driven purely by income tax and transaction cost considerations, because you can always sell, and then buy again. Additional references for the valuation — and reserving — of Seg fund guarantees are the two papers by P. Boyle, M. R. Hardy, and C. Bilodeau in the Fall 1997 issue of the journal *Insurance: Mathematics and Economics.*

CHAPTER 4

International Diversification

This chapter is based on a paper I presented at the 1998 meeting of the Academy of Financial Services in Chicago, entitled "Space-Time Diversification: Which Dimension Is Better?" The basic idea — inspired by the work of A. D. Roy in the 1950s — is to compute the shortfall probability for various holding periods and time horizons. Both dimensions reduce risk, but the marginal benefit depends on the current size and holding period of your portfolio. The question of international diversification — vis-à-vis the magnitude of the equity risk premium — is a very contentious one in the academic literature. It is not very clear (a) which is more important, sector or economy; and (b) whether survivorship bias and data snooping confound the results. For other interesting references, please see the paper by P. Jorion and W. Goetzmann in the 1998 *Journal of Finance,* entitled "Global stock markets in the 20th century." See also the paper by S. R. Das and R. Uppal in the Spring 1998 issue of *Canadian Investment Review* and the general discussion of international investing, from a Canadian perspective, in the Summer 1996 issue of *Canadian Investment Review.* The academic literature on international diversification is enormous, and no amount of references can do it justice, but the above citations represent a good start, if you are interested.

CHAPTERS 5 AND 6

What's So Wonderful About Index-Linked GICs? / Can You Cook Downside Protection at Home?

These two chapters are based on a research paper I wrote with Sharon Kim about the relative value and appeal of certain index-linked GICs. The actual paper was published in the Fall 1997 issue of *Financial Services Review*, under the title "The value per premium dollar of index-linked GICs: some Canadian evidence." Originally, the purpose of the paper was to rank the best ILGICs available in Canada, a largely futile and certainly contentious endeavour given the rapidly changing specifications and assumptions. Among other things, though, the paper does argue that ILGICs have an implicit management expense ratio (MER) that is comparable with mutual funds, and should not be ignored. This expense can be estimated by reverse-engineering the embedded options and comparing the results with a strip bond. The difference between the two values represents the implicit MER. Of course, there are serious methodological issues to confront when choosing an appropriate volatility term structure. As well, it is highly unlikely that the average small investor will ever be able to acquire a forward-starting arithmetic Asian option on the MSCI (the Morgan Stanley Capital International) index. Clearly, the concept of baking-at-home would only work with exchange-traded options, and would be very sensitive to transaction costs. Nevertheless, my main message is that downside protection, which is all the ILGIC provides, can be obtained from many other sources.

Please note: In all likelihood, as of December 31, 1998,

the TSE35 and TSE100 indices will have been superseded by a new SP/TSE/60 index. The old indices will continue to operate for a few more years, mostly for the sake of the index-linked GICs whose returns are linked to these same indices. Presumably, the next generation of ILGICs will be linked to this new and improved index. Also, the two-year options described in this chapter are alternatively known as Long-term Equity AnticiPation Securities (LEAPS, for short). However, they may not be available (exchange-traded) for the right maturity, on all indexed products; but over-the-counter, the wizards of Bay Street will sell you anything . . .

CHAPTER 7
Borrowing to Invest

This chapter is not based on any academic paper or active research work. It's a simple and straightforward look at the concept of borrowing to invest. Tax is emphasized because of the substantial advantages to leverage when the interest payments are tax-deductible and the interest gains are tax-sheltered. Unfortunately, many online mortgage/RRSP calculators available in the market today seem to be misleading and erroneously coded.

CHAPTER 8
Asset Allocation at Retirement

This chapter is based on a series of very popular and award-winning research papers I have written with Professor Kwok Ho and Professor Chris Robinson (both colleagues of mine at York University) on the optimal trade-off between risk and return during retirement. Excellent sources for further information are papers entitled "How to avoid out-living your money" (Fall 1994 issue of *Canadian Investment*

Review) and "Asset allocation via the conditional first exit time" (July 1997 issue of *Review of Quantitative Finance and Accounting*). An additional source is the highly acclaimed *Personal Financial Planning*, a textbook by Kwok Ho and Chris Robinson, published by Captus Press Inc. Initially, the research was conducted using the Monte Carlo computer simulation described in the chapter. Much later, I was able to obtain a semi-analytic solution to the shortfall probability using the Reciprocal Gamma distribution. The results of this process are reported in my paper "Is your standard of living sustainable during retirement? Ruin probabilities, Asian options and life annuities," available through the U.S.-based Society of Actuaries. I must, however, stress that our shortfall perspective is only one possible approach for allocating assets during retirement. I would discourage a formulaic application of the optimal retirement allocation — searching for the one that gives the lowest starvation odds — without examining the many other relevant factors, including but not limited to simply reducing levels of consumption.

CHAPTER 9

Your RRSP Saving Years Are Over

This chapter is based on a paper I published in the September 1998 issue of the *Journal of Risk and Insurance*, entitled: "To annuitize or not to annuitize?" The paper, although somewhat technical and mathematically cumbersome, presents a series of computer simulations that examine the odds of beating the mortality-adjusted rate of return from a life annuity. The results contained in that paper, however, are reported conditional on survival (this was forced upon me by an unyielding reviewer), so they uniformly overestimate what I call the true odds of shortfall. In any event, the idea is the same. As per the technicalities, the continuous time mortality rates were taken from a Gompertz distribution that was fitted to the dynamic Statistics Canada and the 1996 SOA Individual Annuity Mortality table projections. Please note the distinction between expectation-of-life and median life. The median life numbers in the chapter were obtained by computing the 50% point on the above-mentioned Gompertz distribution. In any event, and with the usual caveats, I believe people should keep their options open, and defer annuitization as long as possible. Although finance theory has yet to price the irreversibility premium in a fixed-life annuity, it certainly has value. Furthermore, in a recent paper of mine with Narat Charupat and Hans Tuenter, ("The market for fixed and variable life annuities and its effect on risk-taking behavior"), we document the substantial benefits that can be obtained from purchasing variable as opposed to fixed-rate annuities at retirement. This product — so far — is not very popular or widely available in Canada.

CHAPTER 10

What Is a Risky Future?

The question of how to define financial risk is the subject of an ongoing debate among finance academics and practitioners. The most vocal and prominent opponent to time diversification and shortfall as a measure of risk is the Nobel laureate, Professor Paul Samuelson, at MIT. Please see my Schulich School of Business working paper entitled "In defense of shortfall as a rational measure of risk" for a detailed discussion of this issue. In any event, the following books are excellent for further reading on risk, regret, and the stock market.

Peter Bernstein. *Against the Gods: The Remarkable Story of Risk.* Toronto: John Wiley and Sons, 1996.

Ron Dembo and Andrew Freeman. *Seeing Tomorrow: Weighing Financial Risk in Everyday Life.* Toronto: McClelland and Stewart, Inc., 1998.

Burton G. Malkiel. *A Random Walk Down Wall Street.* New York: W.W. Norton and Company, 1996.

Jeremy J. Siegel. *Stock for the Long Run: A Guide to Selecting Markets for Long-Term Growth.* Concord, ON: Irwin Professional Publishing, 1994.

A final note: If you want to share your views on risk — or if you would like to hear more of mine — feel free to contact me at moneylogic@netscape.net.